# Book 6

# WAR
# IN
# THE INDIES

*The Dutch in Wartime*
*Survivors Remember*

*Edited by*

# Anne van Arragon Hutten

Mokeham Publishing Inc.

**The Dutch in Wartime Series**
*Book 1 - Invasion*
*Book 2 - Under Nazi Rule*
*Book 3 - Witnessing the Holocaust*
*Book 4 - Resisting Nazi Occupation*
*Book 5 - Tell your children about us*
*Book 6 - War in the Indies*
*Books 7, 8 and 9 will cover Operation Market Garden,*
*the Hunger Winter and Liberation.*

© 2013 Mokeham Publishing Inc.
Box 20203, Penticton, B.C., V2A 8M1, Canada
PO Box 2090, Oroville, WA, 98844, USA
www.mokeham.com

Cover photograph by Sanne Terpstra

ISBN 978-0-9868308-7-7

# Contents

*On the front cover*

The 'Monument for the Indies' in The Hague was erected to remember the civilians and soldiers who suffered in the Dutch East Indies during World War II. Seventeen bronze figures, men, women, and children, convey the misery that was caused by the Japanese occupiers.

The grating behind the statues symbolizes both the sense of community of the victims and the fencing behind which they were incarcerated.

Engraved in the base of the monument are a map of the Dutch East Indies, and the following text:

*8 Dec. 1941 - 15 Aug. 1945*
*The spirit conquers*
*Second World War*
*Dutch Indies*

The monument was created by Jaroslawa Dankowa and unveiled on August 15, 1988.

# Introduction

*Anne van Arragon Hutten*

One contributor to this book told me that the
Japanese concentration camps in Indonesia
were not as bad as the German concentration
camps. They were not death camps, she rightly pointed
out, and it's useful to note that distinction. In other
ways, however, the Japanese camps may have been just
as bad or, at times, even worse. The cruelty of guards
was everywhere; punishments for minor infractions
were inventively sadistic; the deprivations were almost
as bad.

In the German camps, with the horrendous exception
of Jewish people, children were not usually imprisoned.
In Indonesia, all Dutch expatriates were sent to
camps. This left children of all ages at the mercy of the
oppressor. Conditions were so bad that many, many
survivors have refused to discuss the camps ever since.
When Tom Bijvoet of De Krant requested first person
war stories, there was a notable scarcity of stories about
Indonesia. Not because these survivors did not exist,
but because so few have been able to bring themselves
to write down their experiences.

From another contributor I heard how her brother
resolutely refused to speak of the camp in which they
were interned. Not until he was well along in life did he
finally break down to tell her, in tears, about having been
raped, as a boy, by a Japanese guard. In the camps there
was no court of appeal. Prisoners could only endure,
while hoping for a distant liberation. That some of them

managed to create social ties and friendships and even stage some entertainment at times, is a testament to human survival skills.

Descriptions of the food supply in Japanese camps sound eerily familiar to anyone familiar with the Hunger Winter in Holland, while the sleeping quarters in Japanese camps resembled the primitive shelving found in German camps. Cramming an impossible number of people into a limited amount of space became a finely honed art. Slave labour, physical and mental abuse, and slow starvation through a grossly inadequate diet were common themes. Both in German and in Japanese camps, brutal repression kept large numbers of people under tight control.

In Holland, the war had begun on May 10, 1940 and ended on May 5, 1945. For those living in the Dutch East Indies, invasion by the Japanese began in January, 1942, with the Japanese empire wanting Indonesia's rich oil reserves for their own war efforts. The collapse of the War in the Pacific and capitulation by the Japanese, did not happen until August 15, 1945. Even then, oppression by the Japanese was merely exchanged for danger from the Merdeka, freedom fighters wanting their country released from Dutch colonial rule. Although Sukarno eventually emerged as the main leader, no rule of law existed in the immediate postwar months, and Dutch citizens were often shifted from camp to camp in an effort by Allied forces to keep them safe. Not until a frequently hazardous trip to ships in the islands' seaports did repatriation back to The Netherlands begin.

Those who survived the camps did so only with their lives, malnourished and in tatters. A stop, usually in some Middle East port, was required in order to obtain presentable clothing for their introduction to Dutch civilian life. Once in Holland, they were not exactly welcomed warmly by a country still reeling from its own years of deprivation and oppression.

The majority of those who repatriated to The Netherlands were Eurasians, the product of intermarriage between Dutch colonials and Indonesian natives during 400 years of colonialism. Known as Indos, they were considered to have the Dutch nationality. These represented more than two-thirds of the almost 300,000 who came to Holland after the war. The other third consisted of Dutch people born in The Netherlands.

For the sake of a historic record, we are grateful to those camp survivors who shared their story of wartime life in the Dutch East Indies.

# Historical Background

*Tom Bijvoet*

The Dutch interest in the East Indian archipelago started with the foundation of the Dutch East India Company (VOC) in 1602. The company received a monopoly on trade with Indonesia and set up its headquarters on Java, in Batavia (modern-day Jakarta).

The VOC was not interested in land ownership, strictly focusing on trade. When repeated attempts to persuade Dutch women to move to Java failed, the company started to encourage its officials to marry native women. Thus, a mixed 'Indo-European' culture evolved.

In the 18th century the fortunes of the VOC declined and in the early 19th century the Dutch government took over the administration of Java, governing through the mediation of native Javanese nobility. In the course of the 19th century colonial culture became more European and the mixed culture was under threat. The Dutch colonial authorities took control of all areas of the archipelago, by force where necessary and started to promote private initiative. This led to the proliferation of profitable plantations producing palm oil, rubber and tobacco. The outlying islands gradually became more profitable than Java; Sumatra in particular experienced significant economic growth. A traditional colonial society of wealthy planters evolved. The welfare of the native population became more important to the Europeans and education, health care and labour laws improved, be it in the Euro-centric paternalistic fashion typical of the era. The same circumstances spawned an independence movement led by young native intellectuals.

After Germany invaded The Netherlands in 1940, the Dutch East Indies remained under Dutch control until the Japanese invasion of 1942. The Royal Dutch Indian Army (KNIL) was defeated quickly and the Japanese started to foment fervour for independence.

Dutch prisoners of war (POWs) were deployed as slave-workers for the Japanese authorities and Dutch citizens as well as Indo-Europeans were incarcerated in camps, the men separate from the women and children. The POWs were treated inhumanely and deployed in work projects such as the infamous Burma Railway. Treatment was so harsh that 8,200 POWs, 20% of the total number, did not survive the war and those who did were physical wrecks when peace came. Circumstances in the civilian camps were better, but not much. There was a chronic shortage of food, water and medicines and the camp guards meted out cruel punishments for minor infractions. Dysentery, malaria and other diseases were common while the severe tropical heat intensified the suffering. About 16,000 civilians died, 8% of the total.

On August 15, 1945 Japan capitulated and on August 17 the nationalists proclaimed independence. The power vacuum resulted in a bloody period of anarchy and retribution in which thousands were killed. Most civilian inmates remained in the camps, ironically mainly for their own safety, until they were finally liberated almost a year later.

After negotiations about independence broke down,

an armed conflict between the Netherlands and the Indonesian nationalists ensued and lasted from 1947 until 1949.

A NOTE ON THE SPELLING OF GEOGRAPHICAL NAMES

Before 1947 the languages spoken in Indonesia were spelled according to Dutch orthographical conventions. After 1947 the spelling of the national language, Bahasa Indonesia, was brought in line with common internationally recognized conventions. Major differences are:

| PRE 1947 | POST 1947 |
|----------|-----------|
| oe | u |
| dj | j |
| tj | c |
| j | y |

So Djakarta became Jakarta, Soerabaja became Surabaya and so forth.

In the text we have attempted to use the current Bahasa Indonesia spelling wherever possible for geographical names, to facilitate identification.

We have made an exception for the names of the internment camps, where we generally follow the old colonial spelling, because on the whole that is the way these camps have been recorded in existing histories, memoirs, and biographies. Thus by maintaining the colonial spelling the connection with the historical record remains intact.

# I could never be a child again

*Anne Rietkerk Houthuyzen*

I was born in 1934 in Yogyakarta on the island of Java of Dutch parents, the oldest of three children. While I grew up we had a nice home, my father had a beautiful car, and I had everything I could wish for.

Not long after the war began in 1942, Japanese airplanes flew overhead and bombed our airport, while Japanese soldiers marched into our city. My sister and I thought it was so funny to see these short, stout soldiers strut pompously down the main street, with their sabers that were much too long for them clicking on the pavement. The next day they closed our school and made it into a prison where they interned many men, including my father. That was the end of school for us.

Some time later my father was transferred to another building. I think it had been a military school, now turned into a prison camp, where we could still visit with him behind barbed wire. On one of those visits three men were being executed for having secretly left the camp at night to visit their wives and children. At the crucial moment my mother pulled me away.

We tried to carry on with life as much as possible. Many stores were closed since their Japanese owners had put on uniforms the day the war broke out, and they knew the city. One hot afternoon a Japanese soldier headed for our home, knocked on the door, asked for a drink of cold water and marched right in. He saw my little brother in his crib and closed the curtains. This frightened us, of course, but standing beside my brother's crib he pulled out of his uniform jacket a picture of his family. He pointed to his own little boy and said that he missed him very much and did not want to fight in this war.

Not long after this we were told to leave our home, taking only our essential belongings. Our beds would be shipped separately; everything else was to be left behind. My mother, my sister and brother and I got ready and went to the train station where a very frightening scene awaited us. Soldiers with guns and bayonets were stationed about twelve meters apart alongside the train. As we boarded, our Indonesian servants cried and tried to help us, but were roughly pushed away. We children carried backpacks containing things we needed, with favourite toys tied to the straps. Right there, watching my anxious mother and the crying children, I made up my mind that my childhood was over, and that from now on I had to be strong for my mother. I was eight years old and after this I could never be a child again.

In the train on the way to the prison camp the Dutch women started singing. I could never get over their sense of humour. This was one thing the Japanese failed to understand, and many times this singing was what carried us through.

Arriving in Banjoe Biroe, the filthiest prison one could imagine, we were assigned our places. The Japanese camp commander appointed Dutch leaders who would report to him and be responsible for organization and carrying out orders for the various blocks and spaces. Our family was fortunate to get a separate room for the four of us. The first thing the Dutch women did was to scrub the facilities.

The beginning of our internment was not too bad.

There were about 2000 of us in this camp. We received food every day, although it was only just enough. Early one morning we were awakened by tinkling glass and noticed glass bottles on our cupboard shaking, while we were rocking in our beds. My mother yelled, "Outside!" As we scrambled out we saw the ground being split open at different places, but none of the buildings collapsed. I remember standing there mesmerized, not able to move: this was an earthquake.

A few weeks later a tornado hit our camp. Covered walkways from one barrack to the next were torn away, and I saw a table fly through the air. Again, God was good and no lives were lost.

Our lives under Japanese rule became unbearable. We were given duties such as pulling grass by hand to clean a field, and cutting trees with kitchen knives, under threat of no food at all for a day. We received cooked tapioca in water with no taste at all, which we promptly called 'snot'. A lot of older people and babies died for lack of milk.

More and more people from other camps were crammed into ours. The beds were removed, we lost our room, and instead of beds, wooden platforms were built. Every person was assigned 50 centimeters to sleep on. At night children cried, others coughed, some people fought, and there was not a moment's peace. Restful sleep was impossible.

There were three rows of plank beds (*britsen*) along the three walls of the ward. The door to the wards had been removed. Sometimes the Japanese guards would come in the middle of the night and shine their flashlights right into our faces. Many years later my mother would still wake up screaming because she had nightmares about this. Sometimes the water was shut off for a whole day and there was nothing to drink. Other days we were told the water was poisoned, so we did not dare drink any and that in a hot, tropical country! Every morning we had to stand at attention in rows of five. The person in front had to count in Japanese. We children always volunteered as we thought it was fun to learn Japanese, and we did it with great enthusiasm. After the counting there were three commands: *Yutskay!* (stand at attention), *Keray!* (bow exactly ninety degrees), and *Moray!* (stand up straight).

With the lack of healthy food and cleaning supplies, disease became rampant. My mother became sick with dysentery and then beriberi. Many people had swollen feet and legs because of the hunger. In the end it also affected the mind, and all people could talk about was food. We were graciously allowed to collect and cook Agatha snails. With some imagination they tasted like chicken. We older girls were allowed to go outside the camp under the guard of a Japanese soldier and collect *ketella* (cassava) leaves. After boiling these for three days they tasted a bit like spinach. Sometimes I wandered away and saw a bunch of bananas or other fruit and would hide them in the center of my knapsack. I would put lots of ketella leaves around them. This was strictly forbidden, but I did anything I could to keep my mother alive.

Very early in the morning I would go down what we called 'Canary Lane' to feel the ground to see if I could find any canaries, as we called the big nuts that fell from the canary trees. They were very nourishing. If you went there too late, they would be gone, as other people also picked them up. On one such expedition I wandered away from the guard and came upon an old cemetery where skulls and other human bones were lying right on the ground. As they were not buried very deep, it seemed they had worked themselves up out of the ground. In the centre of this field of death grew beautiful lilies. I stood there for a while, and somehow this gave me great peace.

Our life continued, with hunger, hard work, carrying heavy pieces of wood to the kitchen, picking grass, intimidation, and always the yelling of the Japanese. We could never do anything right. Any time of day, as soon as any Japanese appeared, we were supposed to do the bow routine. If it was not exactly a ninety-degree bow, a beating would follow. On one such occasion two very old ladies were beaten with iron rods. It was hard to watch those scenes.

When the Japanese were in a benevolent mood we were taught to grow gardens. When the tomatoes, vegetables and beans were ready, they came and destroyed our crop in a fit of rage right before our eyes. Sometimes the Red Cross would be allowed to bring in some extra food for the little ones. It was never very much and never for Mom and me, because she thought we could do without.

Finally one day I just lay down and had no strength to get up anymore and said, "God, if you want me to take care of my mother and sister and brother, I have to have something to eat." Mom was too weak to notice, but somebody walked by, saw that I was in bad shape and brought me a spoonful of sugar. Somehow this revived me again.

At Christmas 1944, we found a little imitation Christmas tree and some candle stumps. We lit our candles and the little tree promptly caught fire. So much for our little Christmas.

Most of us did not think we could last much longer, but we started singing, 'Oh come, all ye faithful'. To our amazement we heard men's voices far away answer us with the next verse. This really encouraged us. Many years later at a market in Amsterdam, we met a man who had been in that men's camp, and he told us that when they heard women and children sing this Christmas carol they were greatly encouraged. In those days it was my child's faith in God that sustained me, and although I had many questions I did not doubt his existence. It was visible in other people who had a strong faith. They sat with the dying and raised children who became motherless during this war.

We finally began hearing rumours that something was happening in the outside world. Somebody in the camp had been able to keep a radio hidden. Many Japanese guards disappeared and we were not guarded so closely any more. One day our camp commander climbed on a wooden box and announced that the war was over; that a bomb had been dropped on Japan, and that his country had capitulated. Now he was afraid for his life. We promptly started singing the Dutch national anthem and cheered and laughed and cried. The next day the camp gates were opened and we were allowed to go outside to the small town of Ambarawa to buy food. We were warned to be careful because eating too much after a period of starvation is dangerous. Some people did not listen and became very ill.

Nobody knew what to do next. My father had warned my mother before he left, not to return home if the war should end but to go with the crowd. We stayed where we were. But just to go outside the camp and do some exploring was great. I was eleven years old and wanted to see something of the world.

Our freedom did not last long because fairly soon the gates were closed again, and Indonesian young men were marching around the camp with bamboo spears. They were also shooting at us from the surrounding mountains. These *Merdeka*, freedom fighters, wanted to kill us. We were totally helpless and stayed in hiding most of the time. Before long, Indian Ghurkha troops were sent to defend us.

In October 1945, the situation became intolerable and we had to leave that place. Covered army trucks came under sniper fire and took groups of people to different refugee camps. We felt like cattle in the back of trucks but were fortunate to arrive safely at an old army depot. Other trucks had casualties. The next three days shooting started where we were. I remember seeing flares overhead at night and suddenly could not take any more. I stopped reacting to anything people said or did and just stared at those flares. My mother called a doctor who gave me some pills, and I eventually pulled out of this state. Since the situation had become just as bad as before, we were loaded on trucks again and taken to the next camp, Semarang.

This was an Indonesian village, where we lived in a mud hut. We slept on the ground on an old rug, and when it rained we put tin cans all around our sleeping places. One morning a cow sticking its head above the half door and mooing awakened us. Once I was eating a cookie outside and a Japanese working for the Ghurkhas asked me for one. I felt sorry for him and gave him the cookie, but my mother was angry with me.

Here too the shooting continued. Indonesian villages were bombed, since the Allied Forces thought *Merdekas* were concentrated there. Once again it was no longer safe and we were taken to the harbour by Australians and Ghurkhas and put on a Japanese ship called the Igra. It was not very big and they loaded so many people on board that we had to sleep on deck side by side. Our protectors wanted to get us out of Semarang as soon as possible. The sanitary conditions were very unhealthy but we were used to that.

When we arrived in Batavia, or Jakarta as it is called now, we were taken to a big library where the books had been removed. This became our new living quarters. We tried to celebrate Saint Nicholas on December 5, without any presents. It was not safe to go out into the streets. Even in our building shooting could start any time. One time while having our meal, bullets started flying, and I remember hiding with my brother and sister on empty bookshelves.

Once more this was not a safe place either and authorities tried to get us to Singapore. We knew my Dad was there and still alive in a military hospital. My mother had called the Red Cross in Singapore to ask about his whereabouts and at the same time one of Dad's hospital buddies was on the phone enquiring about us, so the connection was made. We had to wait our turn to be shipped out to Singapore, and when the day came we eagerly went on board and arrived in Camp Irene (a former Ghurkha camp near Singapore that was designated a refugee camp).

Here we were assigned to a concrete blockhouse with window openings. There were only beds strung with rope, no mattresses, but we were happy to have our own beds. For tables we used orange crates and finally we had peace and quiet with just our own family.

Army trucks regularly took people into Singapore and one day we went to see Dad. My little brother who was three when my Dad was taken away ran right to the bed where Dad was, even though there were lots of men. It was a tearful reunion, especially between Mom and Dad. We had to go back to Camp Irene, but visited Dad several times.

By Christmas time Dad was still in hospital, but we were allowed to stay in an empty room to celebrate Christmas together. Here I learned English Christmas carols. It was wonderful to sing carols and not hear shooting and bombing any more. We were all recuperating physically, mentally, and spiritually. The day came that Dad could go back with us to Camp Irene.

Now we were scheduled to go to Holland. There was a delay because of a polio epidemic and we had to wait till this was over. Finally we were put on the New Amsterdam, a beautiful ship. Women and children in cabins, men downstairs. Our cabin was crowded with three families but we did not care. We were on our way to Holland. On the ship were two brothers who had lost both parents. They were our age and they teased us a lot. Later on in Holland, my aunt and uncle adopted them and they became our cousins.

During the trip to Holland the ship docked in the Suez Canal at Ataka, and we were taken to a clothing depot for the necessary clothing: a coat, a pair of shoes, a pair of pajamas, a skirt and blouse. From the Red Cross we got a little bag with comb, toothbrush, toothpaste, barrettes for our hair, and soap. There were even pastries and cookies and lots of amusements. It was strange to be a child again and to have fun. We did not know how to do that anymore.

In Holland, we were enrolled in school and found that we were four years behind. The children brought us toys because we had nothing. Then Dad was able to get a home in another part of Amsterdam and we went to another school. Here the children called us 'peanut Chinese' because we had quite a tan from the tropics. I eventually went to the MULO, a kind of middle school, then took a four-year teacher training course. There was one thing that bothered me and that was that I never grew much anymore but remained short.

Later on when I was married and became pregnant, the years of malnutrition began to take their toll. I had no appetite and my young doctor did not understand. I would wake up at night with blood on my pillow from bleeding gums. I saw another doctor who treated gum diseases. I had to come for a penicillin shot every day, even on the day of our departure for Canada. In Woodstock, Ontario, where we settled, I received further treatment and was pumped full of vitamins since I still had a deficiency. I worried about the baby's health, since I was in such bad shape. However, she seemed healthy and sturdy; all those vitamins had paid off.

While raising our children I was always afraid of dying young. In the concentration camp, my mother had been deathly ill and had told me repeatedly that, as the oldest of three children, I would have to look after them if she died. I would pray at night, "God, I am only ten years old. I cannot be a mother. Please keep my mother alive."

Many years later I worked in an office as a cost clerk.

Not long after that the office obtained one of the first computers. It was so noisy, it sounded like a machine gun. Since I had suffered shell shock, my hands began to shake and I was losing it. Also, my desk was placed against a wall, and I had looked at a wall for three and a half years. I went to a doctor, who sent me to another doctor, who tried hypnosis and told me I was just like a boiling pot with a lid on it, and the lid had to come off.

Why now? I was more than forty years old. I had made up my mind to be tough, and thought I had coped quite well. However, I began to get suicidal tendencies and thought about driving into a big tree. Everything looked gray and life was only trouble. Pastors could not help me. Nobody understood. My strength had come to an end.

I was sent to a psychiatrist, who not long after committed suicide himself. So much for worldly wisdom. Dutch author Diet Kramer, who had been in the same prison camp, wrote in her book The Homecoming, 'I wonder what will become of these children when they grow up'. She addressed the issue that many do not know how to live any more after staring death in the face for so long. Well, I was one of those children.

Finally a friend of mine took me to a simple country pastor. Slowly I began to open up and tell him everything I had gone through. I also made myself read a book called Women's Camp on Java. I laughed when reading about the nicknames we had given the Japanese camp commanders, but then came the tales of standing in the hot sun at attention all day long, watching beatings, hearing people being tortured, living in overcrowded conditions, the awful smells of disease, and never being alone. One scene especially had bothered me through the years, where a mother was being beaten by the Japanese and her son, about ten, came to defend her and they beat him too. The author of this book said that although she was not of the same faith as other people in the camp, she had to admit that God was in the camp.

One time I was leaving an international gathering when I saw a young woman looking for a seat. I pointed her to mine and asked what nationality she was. She was Japanese. I told her that I had been a prisoner of war under the Japanese in World War ll, and immediately she said, "Oh, forgive us please. Please forgive us." I thought, "You poor child, you were not even born yet, and you ask me to forgive you." Something in me broke that moment, and I realized that I had unconsciously been waiting for fifty years for that moment when one Japanese would ask me for forgiveness. Now I was free.

Many of us kids were traumatized by what happened to us and many people I have talked to are still suffering. People try to bury these things like my parents did, but in the end that does not work.

# When you're hungry you will eat anything

*Anton Audretsch*

The first Japanese troops landed on Java in March 1942. They landed about 200 kilometers south of my birthplace, Medan, Sumatra. I saw the first Japanese soldiers in the afternoon, coming down our street on requisitioned bicycles and with guns on which flashlights had been tied. They came without supplies, living off the land, which is why, I think, they were able to spread themselves over the whole of the island so quickly.

After one month all the civilian Europeans except Swiss nationals were interned in camps. Men and boys of sixteen and up were separated from the women. Men who were needed to keep the electrical, gas, and water systems working were interned in a former Catholic girls' school; women and children in a separate suburb of Medan, three or four families to a house.

Because my father had a government job we were interned as a family at first. My father lost his job in June 1943, when we were sent to a camp. This was on the Belanan Estate, a tobacco plantation.

My mother was taken to Poeloe Brajan, a residential quarter of Medan, to live in a women's camp. She stayed there until 1945 when she was moved to yet another camp, 250 kilometers southeast of Medan.

In October 1944, my father and I spent three days on a train going to Rantau Prapat, about 300 kilometers southeast of Medan, where we stayed until the end of the war. This camp was in the middle of the jungle, 25 kilometers from the nearest hamlet. It consisted of nine barracks made out of braided bamboo with a roof of leaves. The camp lay on the Kila river, which supplied all our water needs. Latrines were little houses with two horizontal boards mounted above a big rectangular hole, with an outlet to the river via a small ditch. A daily tropical rain provided regular flushing of the system, the sewage washing into the river down from where we bathed.

Over the years our rations had dropped until we received 300 to 400 calories per day from the Japanese. For some months I spent time with a local man, fishing for freshwater turtles, which would be taken to the camp kitchen. A 70 kilogram turtle yielded 25 to 30 kilograms of meat. We were allowed to keep the head, neck, and shell, which were divided between the other man and me. This made about twenty liters of 'soup' that was shared with family and friends.

We also tried to catch the bush rats that ate our olbi rambat, a kind of plant root that we used. They ran across the frame of our barracks at night, looking for food. We ate them too; when you're hungry you will eat anything. Snakes were not safe from our frying pans either; they taste like chicken. They had to be thicker than two or three centimeters or there would hardly be any meat on them. In our camp of two hundred men and boys, four or five died every day during the last months of the war.

On August 31, 1945, the Japanese commander told our two Dutch camp leaders that the war was over. This was two weeks after the official end of the war in the Pacific! Two days later we received the first food drops from Liberator bombers that had flown out all the way from Sri Lanka. Two weeks after that we were taken by train back to Medan, only to disappear into yet another camp. Now we were guarded by Japanese soldiers again, who were under American orders to protect us from danger. In December they were replaced by Ghurkha troops, who were to protect us from the war for Indonesian independence that had broken out right after the end of World War ll. It was mostly youths who were rebelling. The older generation of Indonesians didn't seem to mind the Dutch colonial system so much.

Sure, there had been abuse, mostly around 1930. Since then the system of government had changed. There were new laws; you could not hit your Indonesian servants, for instance, as any offense carried a considerable fine. Much depended on how you treated the Indonesians. My parents taught me early to be polite to everyone. Never order, but ask, I was told. Dad reaped the rewards of his humane treatment of everyone during the war, when he, a smoker, would find cigarettes in his bureau drawers long after all our money had been taken away from us.

Not until March 12, 1946, my mother and I were repatriated to The Netherlands on board the M.S. Tjisadane. There we found shelter with my sister who had been there all along. That was the end of my war years, when I, as a teenager, learned a lot about human nature. Through all this I found myself much older in my outlook than my peers in Holland. I learned much in those three war years, but would never want to go through that again.

# We slept in bamboo huts

*August C. Pijma*

**W**hen my father died in 1934, I was four years old and my brother George was five. We were taken to a Catholic orphanage run by Dutch brothers in Probolinggo, East Java. Some time after the Japanese invasion in 1942, the brothers were sent to a prison camp and the orphanage was closed. All the boys were sent to live with different families. George and I were sent to live with Pieter and Noes Lacerff and their daughters, Co and Ria, in Malang. Noes was our half-sister, and Pieter was our legal guardian. We stayed with them until after the war.

We were all aware that we were considered enemies of the country, as were all Europeans and Indo-Europeans outside the concentration camps. The Indonesians did not trust us, nor did the Japanese. I could not understand that from the Indonesians. This enemy thing bothered me since my mother was Indonesian, as was my best friend, Toontje Soemardie, and so were the servants.

Before the war, race made no difference to me although I did know the different races. Now I was made aware of this issue, and slowly realized that I did not belong to this country that was my home. I decided that when I grew up I would leave and move to Holland or somewhere else.

In Malang I was told to call the Japanese 'Nipponners' and the natives 'Indonesians', with Sukarno as their leader. I was also forbidden to speak Dutch in public and had to use the Indonesian language, Malay, even when I spoke with George, Ria and Co. When I was four I had had to learn Dutch at the orphanage, and now at thirteen I had to speak Malay. Slowly I realized that the Indonesians hated the Dutch and wanted to be independent. I personally took it very hard.

The hate for the Dutch and the Allies was so severe that on public occasions such as parades, there were public burnings of effigies of governor Van der Plas of East Java, who fled to Australia and also of President Roosevelt and Winston Churchill. I know exactly how the Jews of Germany felt when Hitler declared them to be enemies of the Reich after generations of their families had lived in Germany.

In 1944 all Indos, as the Indo-Europeans outside the concentration camps were called, were told to form neighbourhood committees so that they could be more easily controlled by the Japanese.

In Malang we had to go to the Technical High School on Java Street. This was for boys only and ran from 8 a.m. until noon. We called it the 'Nippon school'. There we were served breakfast before singing the Japanese national anthem, the *Kimigayo*, while the Japanese flag was raised. We then had to bow to the Japanese emperor in Tokyo, to the northwest of us. We learned Indonesian and Japanese, and Japanese songs taught by two Indonesian teachers. After the flag raising we had *Taiso*, Japanese calisthenics, to radio music. *Taiso* was broadcast all over Java at that particular time.

Even our clock was changed to Tokyo time, which was one and a half hours ahead of Java time. Hence 6:00 a.m. became 7:30 a.m. ridiculous! We were forced to keep a Japanese flag in the house so that on Japanese feast days, such as the emperor's birthday, we could fly the flag. There were some nice Japanese people living in our street, whom we called the good Nippons, and who talked and joked with us in Indonesian. There were also some Indonesians in Malang who remained loyal to the Dutch, and with whom we spoke Dutch, but even they had to be very careful. They warned us that there were spies everywhere.

Ria, George, and I sold pineapple tarts in the morning for Miss Gijsberts who lived nearby. We got ten percent of the proceeds. It was a nice way to get some money when the Nippon school was closed due to lack of funds. Later, George and I worked for a German national, Mr. Rohmer, who owned apple orchards in Srihowo, Batu Sissir outside the city of Batu. Batu is a resort town in the mountains around Malang. Besides the apple orchards, Mr. Rohmer also had twenty-five 'wives', so I was told. They were all Javanese women. I saw four of them in Srihowo, and they were extremely beautiful. He also had a very beautiful daughter by one of his wives in Malang, named Marsini. She became the wife of a Japanese officer of the Kempeitai, the Japanese military police. The *Kempeitai* had the reputation of being very cruel. All of Malang, including the Indonesians, was afraid of them, as they used torture to get confessions.

In Srihowo we met our old friends from the orphanage of Probolinggo and we felt at home again. We slept in bamboo huts, four to a hut. We had to dig latrines in the open and walk half an hour to bathe in the river. The work there consisted of digging holes for the apple trees, for the big boys, while smaller ones like George and I carried water from the wells to water the plants. We were forbidden to eat the apples, which were grown for the *Kempeitai*. If someone got caught eating or stealing an apple he would be severely beaten. The heihos, Indonesian soldiers serving with the Japanese, guarded us.

Every three weeks we had a weekend off to go see our relatives in Malang. We were paid 19 *rupiah* per month for the big boys and 15 *rupiah* for the younger ones. The food was insufficient. We got sweet potatoes for breakfast; rice with cooked sweet potato leaves in hot sauce and *tempe*, which is a cake made of soybeans, for lunch. At night we got a small loaf of bread made of flour and cassava, and water to drink. We were continuously hungry and were often found at Pa Amat's little restaurant where we ate on credit. At night, a native of the island of Madura came by to sell *soto babat*, a delicious Indonesian soup made of tripe. For five cents we got a bowl of this soup, with *lontong*, a rice cake, to fill our stomachs.

Our boss was Mr. Schriff, an authoritarian Indo whom we suspected of spying for the Japanese. We called him, in Dutch, *geschifte melk*, which is milk that has gone bad.

We were later replaced as workers by *romushas*, Indonesians working for the Japanese. They were also sent overseas to build airstrips for the Japanese before being sent home. George and I then returned to Moes and Pappie, as we called our guardians. George got a job delivering blocks of ice all over Malang. His Chinese employer gave him a bicycle with solid rubber tires.

I got a job at a sausage factory owned by White Russians on Oro Oro Dowo, a busy street in Malang. They spoke in Indonesian to me, but their son spoke Dutch. One day the son ordered me to take some meat to his parents, who lived next door, and there I was bitten in my thigh by their German Shepherd dog. I still have the marks, and I am still afraid of big dogs. I worked at the sausage factory until the end of the war.

In the meantime Pappie got sick with tuberculosis. He had been unemployed since 1943 and was selling soap all over town on his bicycle to make ends meet. Moes sold all her non-essential belongings in order to pay the rent and buy food. Co worked for a real estate company run by a Japanese, and Ria worked in a Chinese-owned store.

In 1945 the Americans began bombarding the airfields around Malang. Newspapers mentioned the Japanese losses in the Pacific, and we looked forward to an Allied victory. One day we read that a terrible bomb had been dropped and that Japan had won, but we knew better. Sukarno declared Indonesian independence on August 17, 1945, and Indonesian soldiers who had been fighting for the Japanese now formed a people's army to protect its citizens and guard against the return of the Dutch forces. Later, many prisoners of war returned home, and the Red Cross looked after them. Dutch airplanes dropped leaflets urging us to remain calm.

The Indonesians declared us enemies again and boycotted all the Indos. It was a trying time and it convinced me that we Indos were pariahs who did not belong in Indonesia any more. Pappie got sicker every day until Moes told me to call Father Singih, the only priest in town. He was a Javanese Carmelite educated by the Dutch. He raced to our house by bicycle and I followed, only to find that Pappie had died. We buried him the following afternoon at Soekoen cemetery outside Malang.

A month later, November 1945, the Indonesian military and police ordered all Indos to pack up and move into a neighbourhood that had been converted into a concentration camp. We never saw our house again. We stayed in that camp until the following June. George and I belonged to a group of boys who did the hard work such as moving people around and transporting food to distribution centers. One day we were caught bartering for food with Indonesian vendors, and the police put us in jail for two days.

The British and Indonesians agreed to evacuate all Dutch citizens from Indonesian territory to British enclaves such as Surabaya, Semarang, Batavia, and Bandung. We traveled twenty-two hours by train to Surakarta, with all train windows closed. Then we were transported by airplane to Semarang, where we saw the Dutch flag for the first time after four years of the Nippon flag. We were put in a camp, a converted school, were deloused with DDT and registered. Meanwhile, Moes, Co, and Ria were flown directly to Batavia on a different plane.

In Semarang we received a new set of clothing and a box of canned food, were put on a British navy ship and sailed to Batavia. There we were put in the Tjideng camp for ten days. I saw most of my friends from Malang going to Holland to continue their schooling. I envied them because there was no way for an orphan like me to go to Holland to finish school. We found Moes, Co, and Ria at the Kramat camp in Batavia, but two days later they were gone. We later found them back in Bandung, in the Merdeka camp. There we tried to resume our lives amongst the Dutch in Bandung.

# I remember when they dropped the atomic bomb

*Beatrix Zeeman Chamberland*

I am the youngest of eight children. My father was unable to find a job in Holland, so the government found him a job in Indonesia. Only my two oldest sisters were born in Holland, the rest of us all in Indonesia. At first my parents lived on Sumatra. The island had busy ports because so many goods were being shipped to Holland. Some things came from Holland too, like Verkade brand cookies and condensed milk. Many of our foods came in tins, especially tea and coffee. We had a cook, someone to wash the clothes, and someone to clean the house and make the beds. The house was easy to clean with tiles on the floor. We slept under a klamboe, a mosquito net. Malaria was everywhere, and some of the Dutch caught that. We seem to have been tough and never got it, but some of us got tropical sores on the legs. One of my sisters still has a big scar from that. But those were little things compared to some diseases. Life was good for us.

When war came, we spent more than three years in a Japanese civilian concentration camp. My Mam with her six daughters and youngest son in a women's camp, and my father with my oldest brother in a men's camp. I was very young when we were first interned and the early years are a blur to me.

We had to go to the central kitchen to line up for food. Maybe we used those tea and coffee tins to put it in, I don't remember. My oldest sister stole cherries late at night. My sisters tell me that sanitation was terrible; the lavatory was merely a big ditch, until a monsoon washed it away every year. There was no toilet paper, of course, no paper of any kind. People who came into the camp later brought along big parcels of stuff, as much as they could carry in clothing and housewares. After two or three years most of it would be used up or broken.

We heard later that my father and brother had to work outside the camp. They were kept busy picking up garbage, like the debris after bombings. They got so little food that they were seriously malnourished. Conditions were terrible. They ate dogs, rats, whatever they could find. They had the advantage of having to work outside the camps where they had a slightly better chance of scrounging or stealing food.

One time some of them had stolen food. The Japanese found out and had them all lined up. They took one inmate of the camp, a man who had formerly been a Dutch chief of police. They hung him from a tree by his elbows, which were tied together behind his back. The other prisoners were told he would be left to hang there until someone confessed to the theft. The police chief was physically and mentally strong and refused to say a word about who the culprits were. The Japanese finally pulled on his legs and broke his shoulders, and he died.

My oldest sister helped Mam with the children. The next sister had to work, collecting garbage and helping newcomers come in. She also had to take out dead bodies. Some women worked in the kitchen; everybody wanted to work in the kitchen. My sister Claire, who was a very small fifteen-year-old then, had to get right inside the cooking pots, which were huge, to scrape them out. She managed to put some of the scrapings in paper and bring that home for us to eat.

We actually lived in houses in a poor district in a city, a bit of a slum. The Indonesian people were told to get out and we were moved in. Space for each family got less and less as newcomers came in, but we managed to keep a room and a half for Mom and seven of us children, with a tap outside. I remember the tap worked a couple of hours each day. We washed very, very quickly under that tap and would carry home as much as we could in whatever containers we had. Like everyone else, we had brought along whatever useful things we could carry when we were first sent to the camp, including bed sheets. As time went on, the sheets were used to make clothes for the children, who kept growing. My mother somehow had brought along a nice compass, which was my father's, as big as a coffee table, and she managed to keep that hidden all those years.

There was one little boy in our camp, my age, and I often played with him. We called him Andreetje (little André). His mother was very big, and she was slowly dying of hunger. She had a chance to go to another camp where the food was better, so she went, but André was left behind. When we heard that his mother had died, my mother said she would adopt him. However, right after we were repatriated to Holland, an aunt of his came to claim him.

The final months of the war are indelibly engraved in my mind. I remember when they dropped the atomic bomb. People do a double take when I say that, but yes, I do. Although that bomb was detonated a couple of thousand miles away the news of it reached our camp thanks to some women who had been able to hang on to their radio even though the Japanese searched all our belongings without warning and often. The poor food and hopelessness had sapped the women's strength, and except for some children, everybody stayed indoors. The streets were deserted most of the time.

On that day, however, all the women were outside, talking, even laughing. My seven-year-old mind knew something really big had happened. When I finally got my mother's attention I asked her why everybody was so noisy and wild. My mother's exact words were, "The Americans have dropped a bomb on Japan, stronger than anything the world has ever seen before. The bomb was very small, no bigger than a matchbox, but so strong it killed thousands of people. The war is over."

I never saw adults behave as they did that day. Crying, laughing, punching the air, jumping up and down, yelling. My sister Lettie and I went to a hole in the wall trying to see what was happening. The excitement lasted quite a while that day until the Japanese guards started to run after us with bayonets fixed to their rifles. The streets were soon deserted again.

After several months, Australian soldiers with wide-brimmed hats came to the camp to give us little pills. Vitamin C, my mother said. They spoke a language I had never heard before. When I asked my mother what kind of language they spoke, she listened for a few seconds, then said, "They speak English but it does not sound like English." I still get a laugh out of that after all those years. I think they came to inspect us, but they didn't stay.

If I were to write down all the things I remember of those eventful days, it would take a lot of space. Like being repatriated to Holland by troop ship, a voyage of thirty days. We stopped at Port Said where we got new clothes, socks and shoes. We arrived in Amsterdam and laughed ourselves silly at the hats women wore, some very high and others flat as a pancake. Almost one-third of a million people came back to Holland from the Indies, this at a time that was very difficult for Holland and its inhabitants. It is not so surprising that my older siblings remember some friction and unkindness toward us from the Dutch. I myself only remember being totally amazed much of the time and, oh horrors, having to go to school.

After a year my whole family went back to Indonesia where we stayed until independence. My father was a harbour pilot and had to keep working, as he was too young for a pension. The government was still Dutch then. We liked it in Indonesia, not counting the camps. The people were good to us. We lived quite insulated from the rest of the population, in our own compound that protected us somewhat, with Dutch war ships in the harbour. But it got too dangerous when the independence fighters gained power, at which time we went back to Holland. Some years later, four of us went to Canada. Another sister and a brother went to California, two sisters, Lettie and Nel, stayed in Holland. My mother came to Canada later. She lived to the age of 94.

# Forty centimeters to sleep in

*Brita Zeldenrust*

In early 1945, we were taken in trucks to a camp outside Batavia. Kampung Makassar was not far from the city. This was the fifth and last camp that Mother and I were in, from spring until the end of that year. It was a work camp. The buildings were constructed of bamboo with roofs made of palm leaves, the same as the natives' huts. There were no floors, just the red volcanic earth and no doors or windows. Each hut housed 500 women and children. There were 6000 of us in the camp. Long benches made of bamboo were built along each of the walls. Adults had a space 50 centimeters wide to call their own; 40 centimeters for a child. It was not quite enough to lie on, so that we had to lie with our heads by the next person's feet, like canned sardines.

Mother and I were sitting on the edge of our 'bed', stunned by our surroundings, like all our camp mates. Then we saw little bugs crawling out of the woven bamboo. Somebody said: "Bedbugs". None of us had ever seen a bedbug before. They stank. We learned to recognize the smell. We heard that the bugs hid in cracks, especially the pits and creases in a mattress.

Our suitcases were set at each end of the 'bed' to make for a bit more privacy. Under the bed, the termites would have eaten them up. Above the beds, where everything we possessed dangled, rats ran freely along the rafters. Between the rafters the spaces were thick with spider webs. We were not allowed to touch these, for spiders catch mosquitos. The barracks looked like an Arab bazar. Every inch of space was used for something.

The Japanese were obsessed with hygiene and cleanliness. If they took all your possessions away you could still keep your toothbrush. The camp was swarming with flies. We were ordered to catch them, twenty flies per day by each of us and deliver them to the hanchow. She had to count them and cross your name off the list to make sure everybody did their share. The children had time to catch them. Mother and I just put a plate outside with some water in it, and flies would fall in and drown. Within a couple of weeks we had no fly trouble any more.

We did not spend much time inside, however, for we had to work, six days a week, ten hours per day. We got paid seven cents a day. There was a small canteen in the camp where you could buy a few things like tea or curry powder. Most of us worked in the fields growing spinach, for ourselves and for the other women's camps in Batavia. Our camp was a farm.

The day started at six with everybody standing at attention in front of our barracks. We had to line up in rows of five, one row behind the other and stand there until the Japanese camp commander came to count us. The women in front had to count aloud, in step with the commander, in Japanese: *ichi, ni, san, shi, go, sitji, hatiji…* The barrack *hanchow* had to accompany the commander with the list of inhabitants in our hut and the numbers had to check out. If they didn't we had to stand there until they did or until it was discovered why they didn't. Some of us might be in the camp hospital, or sick in bed. There was no excuse for not being on parade. All 5700 women and children, with no boys older than ten, had to be accounted for before we could disperse.

After breakfast we were marched off to the fields, and when going through the gate we were counted again. The children stayed behind; they had nothing to do. There was no school. Marching back into the camp at lunchtime we were counted again and again in the afternoon when we returned into the fields to work and again coming 'home' and for the last time at sunset. Six times per day we had to stand on *tanko*. We learned the Japanese numbers very well.

We worked under the burning tropical sun, without hats. We got so tanned that we looked like natives. Our own camp got plenty of spinach every day. We got some for supper with our meager ration of rice; rice and spinach, rice and spinach, day after day. For breakfast and lunch we got a thin slice of gummy bread. We were terribly malnourished and so hungry, so terribly hungry all the time that food was all we could think of and talk about. All you heard were stories about feasts and favourite recipes. We stole food whenever we had an opportunity.

One wonderful thing was that we had some wise women for camp leaders. Somehow they collected money from women who still had some. They must have come from other camps where the money had not been confiscated like ours had been. Anyway, they got permission to buy beans for that money, kidney beans. These were cooked in the camp kitchen and each hut got its turn. Once every two weeks we got a spoonful of beans. I am sure that we owed our lives to these beans. All the older people died, all the ones over sixty. The children did not grow. They stayed small and had swollen bellies and legs. Most of us had swollen legs and sores. The children were quiet and serious like old folks. They would just sit and do nothing. The had no energy. They did not play.

We were warned not to complain about hunger. Our relatives in our home country were hungrier than we were, so we were told, and the people in Japan were no better off. Yet some women whined, and then the whole camp was punished. We did not get any food for two days and had to stay inside our barracks. We just lay on our mattresses. Apparently several women died.

Then the unexpected happened. At the end of the second day, after dark, rumours came flying through the barracks. The kitchen staff had been summoned to work. They were cooking rice. We all got rice to eat, in the middle of the night. Food! And not tiny portions like our usual rations; we could eat a large, heaped up plateful. While eating it the thought struck me that it could be dangerous or even fatal to eat so much rice, with a stomach that must have shrunk and was not used to being filled any more. The rice might expand and burst my stomach... It was scary, but how could I stop myself from eating? My stomach did not burst, nor anyone else's.

The strange and wonderful events did not end there. The following morning we were all ordered onto the ball field. We did not have to stand in rows as usual. We just stood there in a large crowd, hungry, emaciated, starving women in rags. The camp commander climbed onto a platform to address us. A Dutch girl who knew Japanese, because her father had been ambassador to Japan, translated: "Mr. Murui says, the war is over. Mister Murui says, we are not to show our emotions.

Mr. Murui says, we have to stay in the camp until our men come to get us."

That was it. Suddenly the war was over. Who had won? What would we do now? We had to stay here, of course. Where else could we go?

We did not have to work anymore. We did not go into the fields every morning but let the Japanese guards pick the bananas and papaya and coconuts for us. The strange thing was that they did not seem to mind. They were friendly; they were good to us. They must have been as happy as we were that the war was over. Suddenly we were not enemies any more. It was not long, though, before they were gone and replaced by Ghurkhas and later by British troops, followed by Dutch soldiers.

We did not stand at attention any more. We did get to eat more, but not enough. We began to leave the camp for short distances to walk to the nearby village, where we bartered for food. The Javanese villagers had food but they had no clothes, so I took whatever we could spare, rags actually and came home with six eggs! Six big duck eggs. I can't remember how I got these cooked, but we ate them and we got stronger. Mother, who had been in the hospital barrack, got better. We lived in a blur of events. The kitchen got flour somehow and they baked huge pancakes, which we ate. We ate everything we could get.

We did not hear from Father for a while. Many days we heard loud crying from women who had received the worst possible news: their husbands or sweethearts had died, sometimes recently, sometimes years ago. Our hearts broke when we heard their wailing. How awful not to have known, not to ever see each other again.

Men arrived, husbands who came to take their wives

and children away, sometimes children who had no recollection of their father. Some had seen his face in a picture. One small boy in our hut once asked, "Will Daddy also get legs?" as the photo had been taken from the waist up.

Then we received a letter from my father, written in his familiar handwriting. The father of one of my friends had brought it; he came from the same men's camp. I went to ask him how my father was. The other man hesitated, then answered, "He walks again." Father had been very ill with dysentery for over a year. Put in the dying room, he refused to die. Two teenagers whom he had taught clandestinely in the camp, and who worked in the camp kitchen, secretly brought him some food. They saved his life. The end of the war had come none too soon for him. He had walked out of the camp to a nearby village, as I had done and had bartered his gold wedding ring, the only thing he had, for food. Normally he would have been one of the first to come and get us. When he did not, we went to him.

Of that journey I remember very little. I know we travelled by train. Java at that time was not safe. The big war was over, the Japanese army had left, and the Indonesians now wanted to be free and independent. *Merdeka*! Freedom! was their slogan. It was heard and seen everywhere. There was unrest and shooting and the beginnings of a revolution.

# Living on a dairy farm during the Pacific war

*Cap van Balgooy*

These were perhaps the most exciting years of my life. I'd never dreamt that I would see Japanese people carrying long rifles and swords enter the grounds of our 240 hectare mixed farm, 'Tegalsari', on the slope of Mount Slamet, in Central Java. Our family consisted of my Dutch father, Josephus N.A. van Balgooy, aged 63 in 1942; my Javanese mother, fiftyish; my brother Max, aged ten; and myself, Cap, aged eleven. My father had built up our farm to three hundred registered Frisian dairy cattle as well as a thousand pigs and other livestock.

My brother and I did not pay much attention to the political and military situation; neither did my parents, nor the reigning bureaucrats. Japan was far away and what did a Japanese war matter? They could not even make toys that lasted more than a month, and their ships or boats would sink in heavy weather because these were made out of tin cans. Flying? Out of the question – they all wore glasses!

What the colonial powers did not envision was that the native population would side with the invaders. The Japanese passed themselves off as the liberators of Asia and that clinched it. It is one thing to fight an army; it is something else to fight an entire population. The Dutch colonial army never put up much of a fight.

The Japanese officially occupied the island of Java

around March 8, 1942, but it was not until the middle of that month that I saw the first Japanese soldiers. One day, forty to fifty Japanese soldiers arrived at our farm in Chevrolet trucks. They were a stinking, dirty looking group armed with over-sized rifles with bayonets. Their officers, dressed in dark brown woolen jackets and white shirts, immediately walked up to our house. The first thing the officers did was to show my father a map and ask him whether everything was correct. To my father's amazement that map showed every building, trail, and creek in the area as well as on our farm. Our farm, while extensive, was hardly strategically important, yet it had been mapped in detail and was now officially declared Japanese property; my dad was retained as provisional manager.

My dad was told that from then on he needed a permit to sell his farm stock, mostly to the Japanese, and they would set the price. Fifty percent of the milk was to be delivered to some Japanese office, and the other fifty percent was to be allocated to the former missionary hospital that also had been taken over by the new regime. There was nothing Dad could do about it.

To his astonishment, the officers did not confiscate his remaining hunting rifles at first. One of them inspected the .401 SL Winchester, saying something like 'nice weapon'. Today, that rifle is considered an assault rifle in the US. This was the first time that I saw soldiers armed with bolt-action shotguns. We were ordered to bow deeply for every Japanese soldier, regardless of rank. This kind of obeisance was strictly enforced; any failure was immediately punished by a barrage of kicking, punching, and screaming.

A month or so later, my father's firearms were

confiscated. Later, radios were seized, as well as three of our four passenger cars and one of our trucks. This was happening all over the occupied territory. Practically any communication and travel became extremely difficult and nobody knew much about what was happening anywhere. Afterwards we were aghast at learning how many camps there had been everywhere, not just on Java, and how incredibly harsh the conditions in these camps had been, with starvation and disease the norm rather than the exception.

When the Dutch army started their retreat from the outer islands, hordes of their Dutch inhabitants moved to Java, mostly to the mountains away from the vulnerable coast. Our farm was ideally situated and provided shelter where needed. We welcomed four families, whom we put up in my uncle Michel's empty house. We also looked after other uprooted people. When the males were imprisoned, their wives and children remained behind, as they had nowhere else to go.

Among these refugees were a Mrs. Te Kamp and her son. Her husband was a member of the NSB, the Dutch pro-Nazi party, who had been detained by the Dutch government and incarcerated in June of 1940. He was released by the Japanese and arrived at our farm a little after his wife and child. The Japanese imprisoned him again with all the other Dutch males. This did not end his incarceration for, after being released from Japanese internment in August 1945, the provisional Indonesian government detained him for another two years. That man was a political prisoner for close to seven years. Throughout the occupation Max and I weekly toted bags of food around to the people we sheltered.

Any kind of Dutch education was forbidden; all schools were closed, their teachers sent home. All Dutch private enterprises such as shops and plantations were closed, their employees sent home or interned. Banks were taken over by the new government; private accounts were soon closed and probably confiscated. My Dad managed to open a bank account only because he needed one for the farm. No more than a handful of workers, occupying so-called 'essential' positions such as farmers like my Dad were retained. Not long after the Japanese arrived our Dutch money was replaced by Japanese paper, to be followed later by completely different banknotes and coins with Malay text. These were as worthless as the new aluminum coins.

In April 1942, all local male Dutch citizens were ordered to report to the Japanese military authorities in Purwokerto, Central Java. The entire group was herded to the local school for boys run by Catholic priests, now prisoners of the Japanese. We learned later that not all Dutch males had obeyed this order, and some had gone more or less underground. A score of these, mostly young adults, later worked on our farm, ignored by the Japanese.

When my mother heard that my father had been detained she decided to go to town and deal with this personally. This was easier said than done. We discovered that the school was encircled by a ten-foot high barbed wire fence, with a soldier standing guard every twenty to thirty feet. My brother and I, being quite young, could freely walk along this fence. One day I did see my Dad and he also noticed me. Returning to our temporary home, I grabbed two cans of Retzke cigarettes and went back. Showing the nearest guard the cigarettes, I gesticulated that I wanted to give these to one of the detainees. He turned his back on me and walked away, at which time I threw both cans over the fence, where my father retrieved them. Buoyed by this success, I kept returning with razor blades, cans of food, and other supplies. Several ladies had been watching my actions and at last decided to follow my example. That caused the guards to come rushing up, grunting and shouting, brandishing their firearms, chasing both women and prisoners away from the fence.

All school buildings in the area had been converted to Japanese barracks, providing Max and me with entertainment: watching Japanese soldiers or Indonesian policemen marching, or the Major of the local *Kempeitai*, Cato, riding out on horseback, while we waited to get a glimpse of our Dad.

One glaring cultural difference between Dutch and Japanese, that neither the Dutch nor the local natives could get their head around, was the behavior of the Japanese towards non-Japanese or lower-ranked people. Slapping people in the face was acceptable behavior. Any higher ranked Japanese was invariably free to slap, beat, or kick any lower ranked individual. Similarly, even low ranked Japanese were free to maltreat any non-Japanese, particularly POWs. Brutal physical violence was the norm and could happen at the slightest provocation. Neither women nor old people were spared.

After a month or so the Japanese started to introduce their civilian government. Several Dutch government offices were now occupied by their Japanese counterparts, their former occupants either sent home or interned. Following the Dutch system, they too appointed a 'Resident' for every district,. Except their Resident wielded ultimate power; he was the 'God' of that district. Besides overseeing civilian matters, he also had the power to replace or fire army officers. In our district the new Resident was a man of Japanese-Russian descent, named Hori.

When Colonel Hori was appointed Resident, my father was still behind barbed wire. One of my Dad's Chinese friends, a physician, suggested that Max and I see Colonel Hori and ask him whether my father could go free. Off we went. Walking straight into his office, we asked the guard whether we could see the Resident. An aide by the name of Yamamoto asked us in Malay what we wanted. "To see Colonel Hori". He disappeared, returned after a few minutes and escorted us to a huge room. There stood Hori. When he asked us why we wanted to see him, we asked him if our father could be released from internment, 'because he was old'. I don't remember if it was Max or I who then explained that we'd heard he had the power to release prisoners, at which he promised to give his answer over the telephone in a few days. At that time we still had a telephone connection. If this sounds far-fetched, I should explain that Japanese were known to be fond of little children and inclined to favor them.

Some three days later my father was released and driven home. My Dad had lost twenty pounds in those three and a half months.

Our Javanese farm hands interpreted this to mean that their ndoro, or boss, was not an enemy of the Japanese after all. They appeared in droves at our house to honour

Dad. Later we realized that the Japanese direly needed the products of our farm. There were only two other big dairy farms. Large farms like ours were unknown in Japan and valued for their products in the war effort. While our milk was still trucked to our pre-war depot in Purwokerto, where it was now being distributed under Japanese control, pigs could only be sold to the Japanese administration at their price. We raised our own vegetables, fowl, and small stock and didn't have to share those.

My mother, a Javanese citizen, owned several rice fields. She and all rice growers had to hand over fifty percent of their harvest to the Japanese government. The result was predictable. Soon enough quite a few acres of valuable sawah sprouted corn, cassava, or sweet potatoes instead; there was no levy on those yet.

Colonel Hori subsequently befriended my father. My Dad despised every Jap, as he called them, who crossed his path, but he could talk at length with Hori. I wasn't aware of this earlier, but my Dad could speak French and so could Hori. When he visited our farm he was never armed except for with his treasured samurai sword, which he always took off and placed in a corner of the room. Nobody was allowed to touch it, not even we children. We were only allowed to look at it. Once he deigned to pull his sword out of its scabbard to show us what it looked like. Samurai swords are more or less sacred heirlooms, denoting high rank. They carry great symbolic power in themselves.

Once our farm had essentially passed into Japanese hands, my Dad had to follow Japanese orders. One of these stated that on the 8th of each month all the farm workers had to gather facing due north while a proclamation was read out loud in Malay by the Javanese foreman, ending with the requisite deep bow to the north, shouting '*Kere!*'. In essence, that proclamation reminded the workers that on that date, the 8th, the Dutch government had surrendered to the Japanese Imperial Army and the Japanese had liberated 'Indonesia'. Thus the Indonesian workers had to be properly grateful to the Imperial army for relieving them of the Dutch yoke.

Twice during the occupation we were required to attend a ceremony to honor emperor Hirohito's birthday. Several dozen Japanese officers were gathered on the pasture, waiting for the sun to rise, nibbling on dried cuttlefish and drinking sake. At the moment the sun appeared above the horizon, they all faced east and bowed deep, while the most senior Japanese officer gave a speech in Japanese.

Since all schools had closed, my Dad hired one home teacher after another for Max and me. None of these ladies stayed long before they, too, were interned. Finally my father found a Hungarian radio operator to teach us. Mr. Olah had served on a Hungarian ship when The Netherlands was drawn into the war in May 1940. Because Hungary was allied with Germany, the Dutch had promptly interned him. He was hired to teach us Japanese and English, both of which he spoke fluently. The problem was that he didn't speak any of the languages we two spoke. After a year or two Max and I were able to speak some Japanese and English.

Since our school days were necessarily short, Max and I spent most of our time feeding the pigs or goats. We also tried to protect the farm against vermin and thieves. There were rats, mice, cats, mongoose, civets, monkeys, snakes, and Bandicoot rats as big as cats.

Three unusual events come to mind from these eventful years of occupation. One of them was an earthquake of rather substantial strength, probably in 1943.

The second was an airplane with a double tail and two engines that flew over our area in the early morning at an altitude of no more than 500 meters. It was most likely a B-25 Mitchell. The third event consisted of a telephone call from a 'Japanese officer' who demanded a couple of dozen pigs, adding that the farm was to deliver these by truck. As long as he was shown the correct permits, there was little or nothing my Dad could do except go along with the request. An hour or so later, a Japanese-looking officer appeared to inspect the pigs. However, my Dad's Javanese foreman smelled a rat. Later, we learned that the man had been a Taiwanese working for the Japanese as an interpreter, who wanted to earn some money on the side.

At another time, we housed two Japanese officers, one of them a veterinarian. They were posted with us in order to observe how the farm was run. Neither was armed except for their samurai swords. They were a pain in the neck to Max and myself because we now had to behave ourselves. I had to stow away my BSA 5.5. mm and my Dad forbade us to hunt. They shared our meals, another problem, because they preferred fish and vegetables, and no meat was served during their stay. Fortunately, they only stayed two weeks.

Later again, we had two other Japanese soldiers stay with us, this time to observe our workers. They wanted to see how my father kept the natives in line and whether they actually followed his orders. One of them tried to teach us jiu jitsu.

Towards the end of the Pacific War, late 1944 to 1945, we regularly received other Japanese visitors, mainly soldiers recovering from tropical diseases. One day they asked if they could have some fish. My father duly told them he needed a permit before he could allow them to fish. After some haggling with the Japanese administration he told them to go ahead, but that they had to catch the fish themselves. They stripped naked on the spot, jumped in the pond and caught the fish with their bare hands. This is when I first witnessed a hostile confrontation between Japanese and non-Japanese. One of the soldiers charged our Javanese foreman, Soewojo, to clean a fish, which he refused to do. The soldier made a move as if to hit him. At which Soewojo said, "Don't, or you'll be sorry!" The Japanese, nonplussed, backed off.

By early 1945 it became obvious that the Japanese were losing the war. In May of that year news began to circulate that most of Europe was in allied hands. The Philippines were already back in the hands of the US. Troubles were apparently anticipated for the Javanese chief of police, Supandi, deemed it prudent to post two Indonesian policemen on our farm. These were ex-Marechaussees, Dutch colonial soldiers. Both were armed with a carbine, saber, and revolver. Later, a third policeman with the higher rank of commandant was added. We even went hunting with them.

The Pacific War was officially ended and the Japanese occupation of the islands was over. However, another period loomed, for the natives declared themselves an independent nation, Indonesia. By the end of that August all three policemen were withdrawn, the chief of police instead handed my Dad one Mauser carbine and ten measly shells to defend ourselves. Now. increasingly restive natives were shouting "Indonesia merdeka!" Free Indonesia! During the occupation, the Japanese had diligently taught the native population, inciting them to rise up against the Allied forces should these attempts to reoccupy the islands. Consequently, the Japanese propaganda had primed the resulting revolt, the *Bersiap*, that often proved disastrous for those Dutch who had managed to survive. In late 1945, early 1946 newly freed and unarmed Dutch civilian prisoners of the Japanese, starving and weakened by years of brutal internment, were ambushed and slain in droves by hotheaded Indonesian rebels running amok.

Only after settling in the USA did I realize that I'd narrowly escaped many dangerous situations. Many of the Dutch citizens had been killed by the Japanese as well as by the Indonesians. Those years may have meant the greatest tragedy to the surviving Dutch, for they lost everything they'd worked and saved for in a war and subsequent struggle for independence they'd never anticipated. Our farm, my parents' pride and joy, was completely destroyed and looted in the *Bersiap* period, and we never got a red cent from either the Dutch or the Indonesian government.

# I'm claustrophobic now

*Gerda Pauw Ondang*

I was born on September 30, 1925 in Den Helder. My father was with the Royal Marine Corps and regularly traveled to the Dutch East Indies. He would be there for a year and a half, then come home for one year. My mother never wanted to go because she had five little kids and it seemed too hard. In 1937 she finally decided to come along to Surabaya, on east Java, where the Royal Marine Corps had its base. Later she said she should have gone much earlier because it was so beautiful there.

We had a very ordinary house, but all the Dutch had servants. A couple next to us had five liveried servants for just the two of them. Mom only had three and that with five children. All were local Javanese. There was definitely a class system as in Holland, but not just between the Dutch versus the local population. It existed among the Dutch there too.

When the Japanese invaded the Dutch East Indies it was forced to surrender by March 8. The ironic thing is that my father had been transferred to Australia shortly before that, and we were to follow him on March 1. All our possessions except some pots and dishes had already gone to auction. With the Japanese invasion it became impossible to leave. So there was my mother with five young children and no one to earn a living for her. She was able to collect some of Dad's salary for only three months before that fell apart.

Civilian men were interned first, leaving women and

children behind. In January of 1943 a camp was set up for women and children; it was called De Wijk and was basically a large, luxurious house that had been expropriated from its previous owners. My mother resisted going there while it was voluntary, but by September all women and children were forced to go. There were barbed wire and bamboo fences all around. At first, mother and we children got a whole room.

In November 1943, we were transported to Semarang in the north of Java. We went by train, jammed full of people so you couldn't move, the windows sealed and covered so no air or light could get in. Tropical heat, no toilets, twenty-two hours on that train. We finally arrived in the morning and had to walk to Camp Gedangan. It had been a convent with an elementary school and high school run by nuns. We stayed there seventeen months.

We slept on low platforms (*britsen*) where at first they allowed us each one meter's width. As more and more people came, that space was reduced to 45 centimeters wide. Boys 14 to 17 years old were removed from the camp and sent to men's camps. In September 1944, boys of 10 to 14 were also removed on trucks, with Japanese soldiers yelling and screaming at top volume.

Something terrible happened. The Japanese soldiers asked a few girls to work outside if they were hungry. First it was voluntary, but then they held a general roundup. All girls and women aged 15 to 30 were called up, including my sister Sjaan who was 19, and me, a year younger. My oldest sister, Bep, was in hospital with typhoid fever so she didn't go. We had to go into a room with eight Japanese men. They looked us over as though they were undressing us with their eyes. We were called up again, and my sister said, there's something going on here, so we were careful that time. All of us girls and women made ourselves look as unattractive and sick as possible. By the next call-up, my sister and I had been rejected.

The Japanese came in three buses and took the approved women and girls to a brothel. They were the 'comfort women' for Japanese soldiers, along with the Korean women about whom we read more often.

Food supplies became fewer and fewer, a handful of rice cooked in water. Sjaan and I had to work in the fields, digging up the ground and planting, watched by a supervisor with binoculars. We caught snails when we could, which we cooked in water and ate. Also frogs. Sjaan caught a good frog one time, which she hung in a tree. In that tropical heat it had dried by noon, and she gave everyone a little piece to go with their meager ration.

My brother Cor was in Camp Bangkong, where there were mostly old men. They kept dying off, mostly from beriberi. My brother, who was twelve then, had to help carry the coffins, which were made of braided bamboo. With the heat and the swelling from beriberi, liquids ran out of the coffins as the boys carried them. Cor had to work in the fields too, which was great because we could see him while we were working. When we came back in the afternoon Mom would ask: How was Corrie, how was Corrie? That was what we called him at home.

There was a big fruit tree in the field, and Cor and three of his friends stole one piece of fruit. They were discovered, beaten, and made to stand by the tree in the full sun for one week (to 'dry out'). No food, no drink. After my sister and I ate our meager lunch, we would get permission to go to the latrine and leave a bit of our lunch beside it. Cor would also ask to go to the latrine and in that way managed to eat the little bit we left him. It was terrible. He didn't go to hospital afterwards because only dying people were allowed to go there.

In 1945 the camps were closed and we had to walk to the last camp, Lampersarie-Sompok. It consisted of little houses that had long been condemned for human habitation. We landed in a house with half a front door and no windows. Thirteen people in a house, as big as my kitchen now.

The war ended August 15, although the surrender wasn't signed until September 1. On August 17, Sukarno announced the revolution to gain freedom for Indonesia. My mother could no longer walk and was in hospital. In November we were taken by train and ship to Batavia, a very dangerous trip during the revolution. Eventually we all returned to Holland. Cor emigrated to the USA later and died in 1995. He was the last of those four boys to die; the others all died young. I think that week in the sun did it.

I'm terribly claustrophobic now and always have all the windows open and doors unlocked. That is because of the camp. You practically sat on top of each other and you were closed in with barbed wire and screaming soldiers. You never saw the outside world. When we had to walk to the next camp in 1945, we were weak and exhausted but we got so excited to see the world again. Look, there's a little dog! There's a bird!

I live on the shore of Morro Bay in California, and it's so good to see all that space, and the fog over the bay, and the garden. At Christmas time my neighbours whom

I barely knew dropped in; they said Merry Christmas and brought a plate of cookies. My thoughts went back to Christmas 1944. Camp Gedangan. Sixteen people in a room of twenty by twenty feet. And it rained, it rained, day and night. No comfort, no future. Everything dark. We went to bed, then 70 centimeters of brits space.

Remembering all that, my tears flow freely. I can get by with very little. I love rice and never leave one kernel on my plate. I love to cook, even though I have a problem getting around. I waste nothing.

My thankfulness is so great. The evening is so peaceful. Food on the table, a roof over my head. Peace for all.

# Working in a railroad track factory

*John Markwat*

I was born in 1926 in what was then the Dutch East Indies. Our family consisted of Dad, Mom, myself, sister, brother, and a stepbrother who was in Holland during the German invasion there. Life was great for us until the Japanese invaded Indonesia.

My Dad was a government customs official. He was incarcerated in a special camp, Boeboetana. As the oldest of the family, at sixteen I had to take over the role of breadwinner. My brother Wim and I found a job delivering milk on our bikes, working for the *Melkbron* (Milksource) milk factory in Surabaya.

Coming home one night, we found that the Japanese had confiscated our house with everything in it. All we were allowed to keep was one suitcase. Mom found a house and we moved in. A month later, I was picked up in the street by Japanese police. They took my money, my bike, plus my still to be delivered milk, and I was not allowed to phone home. My mother had heard that all Dutch-looking boys were being transported to the Werfstraat prison. This is the place where I started my three-and-a-half-years of incarceration by the Japanese and later, by the Merdeka, the freedom fighters.

The Japanese were very good at moving people around, and I was in many places: Werfstraat, Bandung 10th Bat, Tjimahi 9th Bat, Tjimani Baros 5, and finally, Tjitjalenka. In Bandung I met my uncle Jan, who had the same name I had. He died, and his name appeared on a Red Cross list. Years later, I think it was November 1945, I met an old school buddy who looked at me as if seeing a ghost. You are dead! he said. He had seen my name on the Red Cross list in Sâbaja. I told him that that had been my uncle.

Also in Bandung, I met Uncle Taris who was to be shipped out to another destination. He was to become one of about 6500 POW slave labourers who perished when the ship they were traveling on was torpedoed by an English submarine. The Yunyo Maru had not been marked as a transport ship of prisoners of war as was required under the Geneva Convention. The prisoners aboard were supposed to work on building the infamous Sumatran railroad that would transport coal to the east coast of Sumatra, from where it would eventually go to Singapore. When the ship sank, an accompanying corvette saved only 680 men, and of those, only 96 survived the brutal conditions of work on the railroad. My uncle died when the ship sank.

In September 1944, I was at Tjimahi 9th Bat where the Dutch camp leader told me that there was a special camp, Baros 5, where doctors, teachers, priests, and other V.I.P. officials were put together. Their sons were allowed to join them. My father had moved there a week earlier. It was here that I saw Dad again after three long years. I still get emotional when I think of how he looked then. So skinny and his legs so swollen from hunger oedema. He had lost more than half of his normal weight. Nevertheless, it was so good to be together again.

But soon after our reunion I was selected to help build railroad tracks, in a tiled-roof factory with a clay floor.

Many were hurt there, and I had a great respect for the doctors who helped without tools or medication. We were in Tjitijalenka when Japan surrendered unconditionally on August 15, 1945, and we were sent back to Baros 5.

Dad and I went home in late September 1945. Food supplies had suddenly improved. We came home on October 1st, but thirteen days later my Dad, my younger brother and I, were again imprisoned in the Werfstraat facility, now by the Merdeka police. This time they were holding us for our protection and safety! The atomic bombs had been dropped on Hiroshima and Nagasaki in August, and I would not be alive if they had been dropped later. But we still had the Merdeka time coming.

We were supposed to be free when the Japanese left. But it was quite different from what happened in Holland after Liberation. General Mountbatten had given instructions that we should stay in the camps until he could liberate us. We did not listen, or we might still have been waiting. We wanted to go home and see if Mom and my sister were still alive. They were! Theirs is another long and very bad, story.

In March 1946 everything changed. We were one family plus an orphan: Fransje, four years old. Mom had adopted her in one of the *Merdeka* camps, since her own mother could not look after her and her father was buried in the Katanabury military cemetery, close to the Burma road.

I think that our beliefs and the will to live, made us survive. A Franciscan priest, Father de Rooy, whom I met in Baros 5, had a great influence on me. He was a wonderful human being.

# World War II on Sumatra

*Peter Vander Pyl*

In the mid-20th Century, Japan had a very dense, hard working population. It had very few natural resources and had to import almost all of its oil, natural gas, minerals and raw wood, which made it vulnerable to offshore powers. Its rulers began an expansion program in 1937 by invading its big neighbour China, successfully occupying major portions of it by 1941. At that point the Allies of Europe, USA and Netherlands East Indies became worried about Japan's increasing power and placed an embargo on oil and steel against Japan. This made their position in China much weaker. The Japanese military command decided to go all out and attack the rest of South East Asia, with emphasis on those countries that had rich natural and mineral resources. To stop the USA from being able to interfere in the Pacific Ocean, Japan attacked the US fleet in Pearl Harbour on Sunday December 7, 1941. They would have been totally successful except for the fact that the three largest US aircraft carriers were at sea. This mistake would eventually cost them the war, because the USA, with its industrial might, declared war against Japan.

For a period of some 300 years the Dutch, who first came to obtain valuable spices, had ruled the East Indies as a colony. The Dutch administrators, business men, plantation managers, doctors, teachers, ministers and so on were accustomed to living in peace, at various levels of comfort, with their many native employees working for low wages, often for decades for the same family.

Life was a piece of cake for the white man with a good deal of racial segregation enforced. My father, Hendrik, was the successful manager of a Dutch trading company located in the city of Medan on the Island Sumatra, Dutch East Indies and also a reserve army officer. Our family also included Mother Greet, sister Rietje, 6, and myself, 8.

Then came Pearl Harbor and within a surprisingly short time the Japanese armies overran most of southeast Asia, landing on North Sumatra on March 12, 1942. By this time Dad had been called up for war duty somewhere in the jungle, where he became a prisoner of war after a short tussle between the Dutch troops and the overpowering Japanese.

The Japanese military had brought civilian administrators with them, the *Gunseibu*, who hired and trained native policemen to be camp guards. All white men who had a job keeping the infrastructure going were segregated into one location and kept at work until several months later when the Japanese themselves were able to take over. The women and children of these men and of the prisoners of war, together with a few men in such positions as medical doctors, teachers, ministers, and non-government administrators, were taken to various locations where there were sufficient, suitable, and easily guarded buildings. Families who lived in isolated areas remained free for some time but eventually they were located and incarcerated also. Between North Sumatra and the Atjeh Region to the north, some forty civilian concentration camps were established with a total population of some 7,000 Dutch, some people of mixed race, and a smattering of Englishmen, Australians, and others; in fact all the whites except for Germans. As time went by the smaller camps were consolidated into larger ones, and by the early summer of 1945 there were only four major camps left in a circle around the town of Rantau Prapat. This was in the extremely hot, southerly jungle area, later described as Death Valley. These were camps Aik Paminke I, II, and III for women and children, and Si Rengo Rengo for men and boys ten years and over.

My own story is mainly about our internment in Camp Brastagi, where Mom, sister Rietje and I first lived and later about Si Rengo Rengo, where I was sent at age ten. Brastagi became the largest and longest existing camp for women, children and a handful of men. It had been a full time boarding school with a capacity of 300 students from grade 1 through high school. Most of them had been children of plantation managers living far away in the jungle. Brastagi was located some 1400 meters high in the western mountain range at the foot of the active volcano Sibajak. It became known as the queen of camps, since it had well-built facilities, electricity and running water, with a cool climate and no malarial mosquitos. The inhabitants got a nasty shock when early in April 1942 some 600 women and children, including us, showed up from Medan to be accommodated somehow. Everything had to be tripled up, with lots of consternation and bitter complaints from the cream of Medan's high society.

Contrary to the Geneva Convention of 1927, which Japan had signed, camp inhabitants were required to pay for their own food. Most women had brought substantial sums of money, since rumours back home had caused a run on the banks. In fact, the Japanese did close all banks and confiscated all money, which went to the Bank of Yokohama in Japan. School management had their own operating funds available and the reluctant 'guest' ladies contributed a portion of their funds, which together were hoped to be adequate for about a year, at which time it was thought the Allies would have won the war

Unfortunately this proved to be incorrect, since the war lasted much longer and also since more and more women were added to the camp, often from a lower level of society, with fewer funds, until a total of 1740 people lived in the camp, squashed together. It forced the camp leaders to cut rations, cut them again and again until hunger pangs became standard, meals were reduced to twice daily and sometimes, when supplies came in late, to one meal for several days in a row. Nevertheless, the women managed to keep civilization going for a long time; amateur plays and music evenings, scout groups and schooling carried on. Initially there was even a daily open market inside the camps where one could buy food from native tradesmen with cash or bartered clothing.

However, the Japanese commander obviously had instructions to make life difficult for us, because bit-by-bit these so-called privileges were withdrawn. Women took to smuggling by going 'under the wire' at night and bartering in the native *kampongs*, small villages, or even by bartering with the policemen at the gates when the Japanese were out of sight. Anyone caught was severely punished, including having to spend long periods in a hot, closed, half high shed in the broiling sun. There were frequent searches of the camp for forbidden radios as well as money caches and jewelry. The ones who suffered the most after such discoveries were the camp leaders, since they were always held responsible. The Japanese had a habit of punishing the so called 'culprits' by hitting them hard in the face several times with open hand, often causing black eyes or the loss of teeth. The native police tended to use cudgels across the back or legs.

When the camp moneys finally ran out things became much worse, since everything had to be supplied by the Japanese. This, combined with a sudden change on April 1, 1944 from having a civilian commander with native police, to a full set of Japanese military officers and soldiers, made bartering impossible and smuggling very risky. From this point on, life in the camp began to break down. Children three and under were dying, older children and women were laid up with hunger oedema, dysentery, jaundice and other diseases. People squabbled about the smallest things; some mothers at the end of their self-control, mistreated or hit their children. The main thought all day and night was food. Diary entries from those days mainly contain references to what had been available to eat that day, which often was not worth more than 300 to 400 calories. As a child I suffered far less, even though children's rations were only 50% of the norm. Small children have an innate ability to accept changes as they happen, particularly when mother says: it's okay, Piet, don't worry.

I remember roll call, where everyone had to line up by the front entrance to be counted. We had to stand motionless, sometimes for hours. Anyone passing out lay there until the commander gave permission to move him or her. The Japanese, as punishment for some infraction of rules, forbade school and Cub Scouts.

Things I remember are the tremors caused by the Sibajak volcano when it was more than usually active and the slaughtering of the occasional *kerbau*, (water buffalo), which, towards the end, was our only source of meat. Once I was awarded the task of holding a pan under its neck, to catch the running blood from which sausages were to be made. That was considered a privilege, because afterwards I could lick the blood off my hands. I remember the midnight disaster when I could not find the bathroom in the pitch dark and caused a racket in the sleeping hall. I got a severe beating from one of the exhausted dormitory counselors. The next morning my mother, in a fury, took me away to stay with her and sis Rietje in the women's dormitory, which was against all rules. There were birthday cakes, somehow made for us by mother from cassava or *oebi*, (sweet potatoes). I once received a slice of bread with sugar during my occasional visit to a very sick old lady, who had traded it for the cigarette she so badly wanted.

At one point the dam of frustration broke and during a few days in November 1944 large numbers of women, based on a false rumour that permission had been given, broke through the boundary hedges and simply walked to town to barter for food. When military reinforcements from Medan finally reacted, the penalties were gruesome and almost took the lives of the two senior women camp leaders, who were hung up by their wrists during interrogation and beaten. Shortly thereafter, in early December 1944 all boys ten years old and up, along with the last few older men in the camp were rounded up and shipped off to the men's camp in Si Rengo Rengo. I had turned 10 in November. It was the breaking point for many mothers, although my own, who had worked hard in the kitchen throughout and gone 'under the wire' numerous times to supplement our family rations somewhat, showed a stiff upper lip and sent me off with a small lunch bag, a smile, and a wave. In mid-July 1945, about six weeks before the war ended, Brastagi was closed and all inhabitants moved to Aik Paminke Camp III in the jungle.

Why were the Japanese guards so brutal?

To begin with, most all armed forces throughout history have been harsh and without compassion to those they overran. In Japan's situation it was also the result of a completely different social order from the one known in the Western world. In Japan's system, the ruling class expected and received complete obedience from the lower classes. Particularly the habit of bowing and bowing deepest to the most senior persons in power, was ingrained. The Dutch and other stiff-necked Western people consider themselves equals and failed time and again to bow or to bow deeply enough. That always resulted in punishment. The same went for any disobedience. If a Japanese commander forbade listening to radios and you did so anyway and were caught, you always paid the price. They also expected that we should unquestioningly obey our leaders. That never worked either. And, finally, the camp commanders were often officers who had failed somehow in their duties and were sent to the camps as punishment. They took their chagrin out on the defenseless prisoners.

While Brastagi suffered, it had much going for it that was missing in many other camps, particularly those in the jungle areas or those located along big rivers, where malaria, dysentery, foot rot, bedbugs and such took an awful toll, and the rivers in monsoon time would run right through some camps. There were also the military Prisoner of War camps, which had their own problems, including the prisoners being shipped from one place to another as forced labour. Large groups of Dutch soldiers were killed when torpedoed by US submarines while on Japanese transport ships in the Strait of Malacca. All in all some 500 prisoners drowned. Their final destination was Padang farther south on the Indian Ocean coast, where they built the Pakan Baroe railroad until liberation day, under conditions similar to those of the Burma railroad.

Si Rengo Rengo was the men's camp where I lived until Liberation day in August of 1945. It was the worst camp anywhere in the Region. It was located some miles away from Rantau Prapat, at the end of the railroad line across from the major river Bila, accessible only by a small hand operated cable ferry. The Japanese had chased away all natives from a large area on that side of the river. The camp was totally isolated with almost no opportunity for smuggling, except for a few strong men who would swim across at night to barter with natives on the populated side. Food was limited to what the official system supplied, what the camp commander was willing to bring in, illegally, for cash payment, or what one could catch in the way of snakes, bush rats and sometimes fish.

The camp consisted of nine *hongs*, oversized sheds made of bamboo with palm leaves for the roof, the whole of it wired together. During a heavy wind it would feel like a boat in a storm. The camp was next to the river, which provided our water (when the gates were not locked for punishment) for drinking, bathing, and swimming. The latrines emptied out just downstream from this area and were a black hole of disease. When the early arrivals brought malaria sufferers with them, the local mosquitos soon became carriers and infected numerous others. Each *hong* was some 50 meters long by 10 meters wide and held up to 224 people on a double level bamboo floor arrangement. Each person had an area the size of a single bed, 75 centimeters wide, plus room for a suitcase at the head, to call home. The entire camp was about the size of six football fields and held 2000 people. When the tropical rains came, the camp was a sea of red slippery mud.

When I arrived there in December 1944 along with some 200 other boys, the ones who had fathers, uncles or other relatives already in the camp moved in with them. The rest of us were bunked together in *Hong* #8 under the supervision of a dozen men, most of them teachers. As one of the youngest boys in camp I was placed next to a teacher. I had no klamboe, protective mosquito netting, at my sleeping place but luckily never caught malaria. The person in the bed next to me suffered miserably from it.

A few of my memories of those days: contrary to the system at Brastagi, everyone, including children, received full rations. However, the double quantities of food helped very little. The old dried out corn kernels boiled in river water, which was the staple diet as I recall, had very little food value and were almost impossible to deal with due to our shrunken stomachs. The diaries I read about this camp show occasional distribution to each prisoner of sugar, salt, oil and coconuts, but I never received any of those much-needed supplements.

I had no one to turn to as substitute father; almost every adult was too immersed in his own misery. For days on end I would not talk to anyone in the middle of the noisy camp environment. I learned very little, was chased away from the cooking shed where those with their own food could fix small meals, was bullied by older boys at the platform from where we would dive and chase fruit coming down the river. My one treasure was the camp library, which I read through from end to end, including material, which was definitely not suitable for a ten year old.

The camp contained almost every medical doctor, specialist and surgeon in the whole region, but had neither quinine for malaria nor proper surgery facilities. There were some 600 boys in camp; only three of them perished. Of the 1400 men, about 120 died during ten months in the camp, in ever increasing numbers during the last few months.

In mid-August rumours of imminent liberation began to circulate, mostly based on the unexplained sudden increase of food supplies and polite attitudes of the guards. On August 24, the news was official, the Dutch flag was hoisted and the national anthem sung over and over. The Allies started aerial drops of supplies, sometimes strange ones. I received two sets of shaving razors, cigarettes, a number of combs and a bath towel. I traded the smokes for food.

We were free, except that we could not leave camp because the Allies did not have the resources to get us out immediately. It took until late October before the camp was completely cleared. I was returned to my mother and sister in Aik Paminke III camp early on. There, lists of surviving military men had been posted, which included my dad's name. To our deep disappointment and pain the next list reported that he had suddenly died a few days earlier. As Dutch military camp commander he had been sent to Singapore in an unheated warplane to report on the behaviour of the Japanese commandants. He died there from pneumonia caught on that plane. After a while we were sent back to Medan and later on moved back to Holland to live with an aunt and uncle and to begin a new life.

# Tracking the past

*Pieter Koeleman*

With getting older, my wife's desire to learn more about her early childhood became stronger. She felt there should be a reason for a lifelong feeling of insecurity. It had changed over the years, but still nagged, deep down, surfacing now and then. She had memory flashes of the Japanese occupation in the Dutch East Indies: prison camps, nightmares, burning planes crashing in the sea, panicked screams. Researching Beja's past, we found that the family had lived in the South of Sumatra, where her dad had a vegetable and chicken farm with a small coffee plantation in an area named The Giesting. She was born January 1940 in Tanjung Karang, a city about 150 km east of The Giesting. Beja's paternal grandmother had arrived from Holland to witness the birth of her grandchild. She had planned to return in April but due to the unstable situation in Europe she had to stay on Sumatra. Her mother's mother and younger brother also lived in the area.

The threat of war was increasing and Beja's dad was mobilized as a reservist in December 1941 and stationed in Tjimahi, close to Bandung. On January 11, 1942, the first Japanese troops invaded the territory of the Dutch East Indies. On March 8, the Governor General signed the capitulation and the same day Beja's Dad became a prisoner of war. That month, Beja's sister, Helene, was born. Beginning in April, all whites, mainly Dutch citizens and Indo-Europeans were driven out of their houses. Families were uprooted and separated. So also in The Giesting. Women and children were separated from boys of twelve and older and the men.

The women and children were transported in eight open trucks to the camp of the Field Police (*Veldpolitie*) in Telukbetung, located next to Tanjung Karang, where they were placed in barracks. Beja's mother with her two little girls and her mother-in-law belonged to the first five families who arrived there, as were her mother and brother. Internees had to supply and prepare their own meals. When they were driven out of their homes, most of the people had been able to take some clothing, pots, pans, some money and small personal treasures.

After a couple of weeks the Japanese moved the internees to the 'Holland-Indies' school where they stayed till July 7. They appointed Mother Superior Arnolda to be in charge of the 350 internees. She was the liaison between the camp commander and camp dwellers. During the day, people stayed outside and during the night they had a spot in one of the classrooms, with more than 40 people to a classroom.

When the next move was announced, 300 Indo-European women and children were released after they had signed a form stating that they were more than 70% Indonesian. Beja's grandmother had advised her daughter to sign the form, but her dad's mother said 'we are real Dutch' so Beja's mother didn't sign the form. Her mother and her brother had signed it and left the camp. The mainly Dutch citizens then carried their belongings and walked to the buildings of the South Sumatran Railway which were nicknamed 'The Pigeon House'. Mother Superior Arnolda continued to be in charge of fifty women and children for the six months they stayed there until February 19, 1943. Then another move followed, to the convent and boarding school of St. Francis. They lived in the classrooms but slept in the dormitory.

Seven months later, on September 27, they went to the Director's house and outbuildings of the Ice Factory. All the locations were surrounded by barbed wire fences. One image comes to Beja's mind, her grandma outside the camp handing a chicken through the fence. That happened several times. Others were buying food from the natives at the gate. Every day some trade was going on. A few native women were inside the camp because they felt safer there. Food was scarce and the native women taught the other women what kind of fruit and plants they could eat. Older children had to look for firewood so the women could prepare the meals. For a mother with two young children it was a difficult time, although people supported each other, especially during Christmas.

On May 24, 1944 the forty-eight interned women and children were transported by train in a northerly direction to Palembang, a city situated on the Musi river at the south east end of Sumatra. There was a large women's camp there, named Poentjak Sekoening, with 500 women and children of Dutch, British and Australian origin already present. Internees arrived from other camps too, bringing the total to 615. The barracks were made of bamboo, with dried palm leaves used to cover the roofs. Plaited bamboo and barbed wire fences surrounded the camp.

The Japanese command was in the hands of a civilian organization, the Gunseibu. The guards were native police and *heihos*, police trained by the Japanese. Internees stayed in barracks, where everyone had their own place on a *bale-bale*, a split bamboo bed, 50 centimeters wide, 180 centimeters long and standing 60 centimeters off the ground. Each side of the barrack held a row of fifty bale-bales. The internees sat, lay down and slept there day and night. No privacy, never silence, never being alone. The whole camp was not bigger than a soccer field with three barracks at each long side.

The open space in between was used for the daily count, sometimes more than once a day. In the centre was an octagonal pavilion called the *pendopo*. At the far short side was the kitchen area, with a woodshed behind it. At the opposite side was the entrance to the camp. Nuns from two different congregations occupied the first barrack on the left side. The other barracks were occupied by the Australians, British and the Dutch, who were in the majority.

In April 1944 the Japanese authorities took over the command from the *Gunseibu*, with a Captain Seki in charge. They started weighing the internees and vaccinating them against typhus and cholera, probably for fear of becoming infected themselves. When the first Red Cross packages reached the camp, they were left outside the gate for two weeks before the Japanese allowed them inside the camp. By that time, most of the chocolate had been eaten by the guards or had simply disappeared as had the Camel and Chesterfield cigarettes. Nevertheless the psychological impact was enormous. What did make it inside were milk powder, sugar, canned meat, cheese, and butter.

On August 11, 1944 airplanes dropped bombs on the

oil installations of Pladju, not far from the Musi river at the bank of Palembang. The weighing of the internees was halted. There was nothing more to eat. The next month they received orders to make themselves ready for transport and take only what they could carry. The internees were transported by boat over the Musi river to the Strait of Bangka on their way to Muntok on Bangka Island, situated between Sumatra and Malaysia. The children had to stay below deck, packed together.

Many people arrived in a deplorable condition and had to stumble with their luggage over the kilometer-long quay of Muntok. The sick had to be carried to the trucks. After 24 hours they arrived in their new camp. New barracks, more air, more space, more green. However the condition of the internees was not improving. Another illness struck, Bangka fever. Patients had high fever for days and often became unconscious and died. More mothers suffered from beriberi.

With more people getting sick, many were not able to carry out such tasks as collecting wood, preparing meals, cleaning latrines. The dead still had to be buried. People became more irritable. Others were lying on their bale-bale, exhausted, eyes deep in the sockets, not responding, apathetic.

In April 1945, everyone had to move back to Sumatra, with destination Belalau, a rubber plantation 10 km. north of Lubuklinggau. Women packed up what was left of their belongings. Trucks delivered the people at the quay of Muntok. On small coal boats they made the 24-hour trip over the Strait of Bangka and the Musi river to Palembang. The Japanese had sent coffins with the transport. They were all used and left on the quay and at train stations. Nobody knew where the bodies would be buried.

The transport from Palembang to Lubuklinggau was by armoured train, all locked up. The stench of sweat, urine and feces was horrendous. Neither food nor drink was available. Only a few had been able to take some food with them for the voyage. When the people arrived in Lubuklinggau in the evening they had to stay on the train till the next morning before they were allowed to stretch out. Some had to be helped off the train, others had to be put in a coffin. During the boat and train trip a total of five women died. They were now 400 kilometers west of Palembang. Finally they were transported in trucks to the coolie sheds of the deserted rubber plantation. Again people were put in barracks, but this time the roof was made of corrugated iron, no leakages anymore. There was a little stream running through the camp used for taking baths.

In April Beja's grandma passed away after suffering from open sores on her legs, any healing made impossible by diabetes. Beja's mom had been sick already for quite some time. Her health had deteriorated, aggravated by giving her own food to the two girls. Beja remembers one of the nuns walking with her to a small shed, where her mom was lying on a kind of bed. Beja had a small piece of baked fruit and gave it to her mom. The next day she heard that her mom had died. She felt bad because she thought that her mom had died from the small piece of baked fruit. It was June 1945, and her mom had died of beriberi and privation. Three years of internment and caring for her two young children had drained her to a point where two months before the liberation her weakened body succumbed.

One evening soon after that, Beja was very sad and cried. A nun took her by the hand and walked outside, sat down and held her close. The nun pointed her finger at a star and said to her: "look at that bright, shiny star, that is your mom".

In camp Belalau, 89 women and children died. Captain Seki was still the commanding officer, infamous for his tough and cruel conduct. He didn't change, but something did. Planes dropped blankets, a much-welcomed gift for the wasted bodies. The guards became friendlier.

On August 24 Captain Seki announced that the war was over. There was no explosion of joy from the internees; many felt deflated. Of course people were happy, some started to sing the Dutch national anthem. The nuns kept looking after the motherless children. The men from a nearby camp came and were reunited with their families. All of a sudden there was plenty of food: unbelievable quantities of sugar, rice, sweet potato, fresh meat, coconut, bananas, even pineapples and papayas. Also quinine and other medicines. Everything for which the people had waited for the last three years was there now in three days.

The nuns moved to Palembang with the motherless children, including the two little sisters. They were waiting for their dad, who had been working on the Pakan Baroe railway, which would connect east with west Sumatra. It took until March, 1946 before Beja and her sister were reunited with their dad, who hadn't even seen his youngest daughter yet.

# Brastagi, Sumatra, 1942

*Reni Wertheim-van Dijken*

**M**y first recollection of the beginning of the war was when I was two years and four months old. My mother was packing things in a galvanized washtub. My father had already been taken prisoner of war. A reddish-brown rubber mat covered the washtub. We were to go to the Planter School, almost across from my parents' summer house in the mountains.

In the beginning we all had to cook for ourselves. To keep the fire going, my brother and I could use a kipas, a sort of fan. My mother promised that we could have one after the war!

In August my next brother was born, and we were promised a piece of chocolate.

We slept on slats over our metal trunks. We had a small portion of a classroom in what was called the 'Baby Nest'. One night I was face to face with a cockroach in bed, and I screamed.

Often the women would gather at night and tell stories, or sing.

What I remember is the tjankol, a bent hoe, with which the women had to turn the soil.

There were two Japanese soldiers. We called one of them Jopie Roeter, and he was mean. The other one we called *Bruintje Beer* (Little Brown Bear, the Dutch name for the cartoon character Rupert Bear), and he was as helpful as he dared to be.

In the beginning the women would smuggle things for food. You were in real trouble if they caught you. There was cruelty: one woman had to stand by the entrance of the camp with her arms raised up high. If she dropped them, she received a whack.

We even had a bit of schooling. We were hungry. I think for the mothers it was terrifying, not knowing where their husbands were and trying to feed their children.

Later, in Holland, I would come home from school sometimes and find a few of the surviving mothers from the camp. They would recall all kinds of things that had happened, and there would be lots of laughter. I think it was one way to cope with the horrendous past.

# Songs of Survival

*Aubrey Beauchamp*

**W**hen the Japanese invaded the islands of Indonesia during World War II, a young Dutch girl, Helen Colijn, lived a quiet life with her family in an oil rich area on the island of Sumatra. Immediately after the invasion, the Dutch blew up the oil wells and then fled for their lives. Huddled on an old steamship, Helen's family tried to reach Australia. Unfortunately, some Japanese pilots spotted the craft from the air and riddled it with bullets. The ship sank and many passengers lost their lives. Three small, overcrowded lifeboats floated aimlessly on the deserted ocean for many days. Among the occupants of these lifeboats were Helen, her parents and her two sisters. They finally reached shore, only to be captured and imprisoned by the Japanese and taken to various concentration camps for the next three and a half years. During those long years, the camp for women where Helen and her sisters were placed, was often moved to different, isolated locations, from Sumatra to Borneo and then back to Sumatra. Conditions at the final, remote location had deteriorated to the point where 37% of all prisoners died, mostly from starvation and tropical diseases. To their credit, during these long years of incredible hardships, the women took care of themselves the best they could, washed and cleaned their threadbare clothes, scrubbed their cooking pots and kept their sparse quarters clean.

To boost the sagging morale, a prisoner with a musical

background, Margaret Dreyburgh, came up with a plan to put together a choir – a choir consisting of the voices of emaciated and hollow-eyed women. She rounded up some potential, albeit reluctant, choir members. After a shaky start, it became apparent that getting together for rehearsals was something these women were soon looking forward to. It gave them an incentive to keep going and a ray of hope for the future. There were no instruments of any kind in the camp so it was only the untrained voices that formed the melodies. After some practice, they began to harmonize, and their voices started to blend in touching and sweet tones. They even gave concerts to their starving and sick fellow prisoners. Even their well-fed guards listened in quiet amazement.

After a year or so, their repertoire was exhausted. All the songs they knew were sung. Then the gifted musical leader, who had directed large orchestras in the past and had an extraordinary memory, had an idea. She remembered the individual scores of each orchestral instrument and, from memory, wrote them down and began to teach her fellow prisoners how to sing the notes of each instrument. It was a unique idea with amazing results. They now became an orchestra of voices, eventually singing works by Bach, Dvorak, Beethoven, Chopin, Mozart and Grieg. These prisoners who daily performed hard labor, who dug graves and buried their own dead, were able to sing individual scores of orchestral instruments. This had never been done before in the history of music. Theirs was music of survival! Unfortunately, the music director was not among those who survived. She, too, was buried in a shallow grave, dug by her grieving, emaciated fellow choir members.

When the war ended, the location of the women's camp was so remote that even the Allies had difficulty finding it to liberate its prisoners. Helen's father, they learned, had died in a men's labor camp. Her mother, imprisoned in another camp, survived, as did Helen and her sisters.

Helen was the granddaughter of Prime Minister Colijn, who led the Dutch government before World War ll. After the war she returned to Holland and, many years later, wrote a book about her years in a Japanese Prison camp called, *De Kracht van een Lied – Overleven in een Vrouwenkamp*, (The Power of a Song – Surviving in a Women's Camp). In the Introduction, Helen wrote: 'This book is about music for voices. The beginning of this sort of music starts about halfway through this book. That's because much had to happen before these women's lives had become so unbearable that, in desperation, it led them to sing. It was the only thing that gave them a ray of hope and sanity. I trust that this book, in spite of the horrific circumstances, will be uplifting and an inspiration.'

Years later, Helen moved to California. The various written scores for these instrumental voices from that labor camp were miraculously preserved and eventually donated to Stanford University in Palo Alto, California. There, someone found them and arranged for a women's choir to perform those orchestral scores again. It was an immediate success and, since then, this 'camp music' has been resurrected to a new life and performed in countries around the world.

Eventually, Helen's book was published in English under the title, 'Song of Survival – Women Interred,' by

White Cloud Press in 1989, followed by several reprints. Then movie director, Bruce Bereford, heard a tape of this extraordinary music performance, recorded during a memorial concert in Australia. "The effect of this music was so overwhelming and sublime," he stated later, "that the urge to make this into a movie quickly became an obsession." He did make the movie titled, 'Paradise Road'. The well-known American actress Glenn Close played the main character. She later said, "Reenacting Helen's camp days was one of the most difficult roles I ever undertook." A CD of the music was produced by Sony Classical and performed by the *Haarlems Vrouwenkoor*, led by Leny van Schaik.

Helen concludes her book with, 'Our music is now liberated and, almost half a century after its first performance behind barbed wire on Sumatra, is bringing joy and comfort to thousands, perhaps millions of listeners in many countries. That's something we, who survived those days, are all very grateful for. Now, memories of those camp days are not just filled with sadness and grief, but we can listen to something beautiful, something real and tangible as a result of those dark years.'

# Thick slices of white bread

*Wouter Hobe*

It was late 1946 when my father, brother and I were released from the Japanese internment camp. We travelled from Bandung to Batavia by train and then on to Tanjung Priok by military transport. I was 13 years old at the time. We were going to be sent to Australia to recuperate. The Red Cross had ensured that my mother would be waiting on the quay when we arrived. She had been in the Tjideng camp. Seeing each other again on the quay at Tanjung Priok was incredible. It still gives me the shivers thinking about it.

We boarded a Japanese tender, as our ship, the Oranje, could not go into the port because of a sunken ship that was blocking the entry. Transferring from one boat to the other was a slow affair. When we were halfway up the stairway we could see through a porthole that everyone was seated at a table eating potatoes, carrots and fish, so I presume it was a Friday.

Once on board we were first taken to our sleeping quarters. I was assigned a bunk with a porthole at shoulder height. It turned out to be the front most cabin by the bow.

Then we were summoned to the mess. We sat at long tables with linen tablecloths. There was butter on the table and cheese and other delicacies such as jam and chocolate sprinkles. When everyone was seated the bread was brought in. Thick slices of white bread. Someone said: help yourself. All of us, without exception, grabbed a slice and buried our face in it. We ate it without anything on it. It was the best cake that we had ever eaten. I thank God for all the blessings that I have experienced in my life. I always bake my own bread and still think back on that first slice of bread on the Oranje.

# I fought in Indonesia

*Herman Bakker*

The war for Indonesia was the largest war in Dutch history, according to an institute that tracks such things. There are hardly any Dutch veterans left of that war to retain this valuable colony, and it's important for the younger generation to hear about it. I will try to sketch an image of that chaotic time. Because of my training at the Cavalry School in Holland and the Royal British Military Academy in Yorkshire, England, I was able to do my bit during 1946-1950 in Indonesia.

In February 1942, the Netherlands East Indies was overrun by Japanese troops. Defending Dutch forces on the islands, then a Dutch colony, lost the battle before long, capitulating against a superior force on March 8. From then on the entire archipelago was controlled by Japanese military troops. The white population was interned in concentration camps, where thousands eventually died. Indonesian nationals and Chinese were not much better off; they were molested and robbed constantly. Many thousands were put to work on the island of Sumatra or the infamous Burma railroad, where many succumbed to slave labour and starvation. Guards, many of them Koreans, were harsh taskmasters who punished the slightest infraction.

The Japanese police, the *Kempeitai*, were omnipresent and instilled fear everywhere. Decapitations were a daily occurrence. Dutch prisoners of war were also put to work on the construction of the railroads, such as the one at Pakan Baroe where more than eight thousand men died.

During the Japanese occupation, Sukarno, who later became the first president of an independent Indonesia, was a willing collaborator and mouthpiece for the occupying Japanese. He was responsible for the four million Javanese nationals who were pressed into service as slave labour. Half of them did not survive the war.

After almost four years of terrible oppression, the war with Japan suddenly ended. This brought new uncertainties. A vacuum of power had been created, and Sukarno stepped up as lord and master, announcing the republic of Indonesia. He began his campaign of hate against the Dutch, and soon the cry of *Merdeka*, freedom, was heard, along with cries of *Boenoch Belanda*, Death to the whites!

This was the beginning of the *Bersiap* period, with the political situation growing more and more chaotic. Sukarno and his forces had a free hand. For lack of other weapons they were armed with spears and *klewangs*, machete-like swords. A few weeks before the first troops sent by The Netherlands came to restore Dutch control, the British command ordered the Japanese troops to withdraw. Some actually refused and remained to guard camp dwellers. It was under this indescribably dangerous situation that the Dutch forces landed. Without permission from the British or Allied forces, they began to battle the rebels. Theirs was a precarious task.

More than 135,000 Dutch troops were sent to the Dutch East Indies between 1945 and 1949. They battled Sukarno's forces as well as a multitude of autonomous native groups that fought for independence and even Japanese soldiers who had refused to surrender. The local population and those in camps were subject to great confusion and murderous events. The Bersiap was in full swing. The Insulinde Corps, many of them soldiers of the Princess Irene Brigade, saved thousands of civilians. They had parachuted into the jungle; a dangerous mission that cost many lives.

Long after Dutch nationals had been repatriated, Dutch troops fought rebels who honoured no treaties or agreements. Soldiers who survived told of patrolling during the pitch dark of night, terrified by the sounds of crickets, fireflies, wild swine, and screaming monkeys. Tropical rainstorms, land mines, snipers and booby traps added to their misery, aggravated by insufficient food and equipment. The constant danger, exhaustion and misery became a nightmare.

Unfortunately, the Dutch police action did not result in peace and order. Dutch politicians had underestimated the strength of Indonesian forces and did not realize they were involved in a total war of terror, murder, fire, and torture, with no borders and no mercy. Orderly troops did not understand guerilla warfare. Thousands of white crosses on Indonesian war cemeteries still testify to the drama of that war.

Nevertheless, we veterans of that war know that we fought the fight for which we had been trained and which was thought to be necessary at that time. Despite the inevitable excesses of war, we also saved thousands of people, fed children, cared for the wounded. We had not asked for this war, nor did the 6,791 soldiers whose remains stayed in Indonesia. There were also 19,000 who were wounded, not to mention a multitude with psychological complaints.

# Contributors

*Anne Rietkerk Houthuyzen* was born in 1934 in Yogyakarta on the island of Java. She was interned in a Japanese prison camp at the age of eight. Anne now lives in Woodstock, Ontario.

*Anton Audretsch* was born 1929 in Medan on the island of Sumatra. He spent much of the war in Japanese prison camps. Ton came to Canada with his wife in 1956 and worked as a geologist for Shell. He and his wife now live in Calgary, Alberta.

*August C. Pijma* lives in Redwood City, California.

*Beatrix Zeeman Chamberland* was born in Surabaya on the island of Java. She was three when they were interned. She emigrated to Canada in 1958 at the age of eighteen.

*Brita Zeldenrust* lives in Arden, Ontario.

*Cap van Balgooy* sent his contribution from Upland, California.

*Gerda Pauw Ondang* was born in 1925 in Den Helder, the most northerly town in the province of North Holland. In 1937 her mother took her five children and joined her husband, who was stationed in Java. Gerda's father was sent to Australia just before the Japanese invasion, but the rest of the family lived through the war in a Japanese prison camp. Gerda now lives in Los Osos, California.

*John Markwat* was born in 1926 in the former Dutch East Indies. He came to Vancouver, British Columbia, with his wife, Coby, in 1956. After running a motel, then a bed and breakfast for many years, they retired to New Westminster, British Columbia

*Peter Vander Pyl* was born in Padang, Sumatra, Dutch East Indies in 1933. His father was a director with an export company as well as a reserve Captain in the East Indies army in Sumatra. Peter came to Lethbridge, Alberta, Canada in June of 1954. He now lives in Calgary, Alberta.

*Pieter Koeleman* was born in Noordwijk aan Zee, Zuid Holland, where he spent World War II. He came to Canada with his wife, Beja, in 1984 to visit his brother on Quadra Island, British Columbia. One visit decided the issue of immigration, and they moved from Holland to Campbell River, also in B.C., bringing all four teenage children along. One daughter moved back to Holland; the other three, with their children, live near their parents.

*Reni Wertheim-van Dijken* was born on Sumatra in 1940. Two years later her family was interned by the Japanese occupiers. She was repatriated to The Netherlands after the war, came to Canada with a girlfriend in 1963 and now lives in Richmond Hill, Ontario.

*Aubrey Beauchamp* is a regular columnist with De Krant. She lives in San Clemente, California.

*Wouter Hobe* lives in Ste. Marthe, Quebec.

**Herman Bakker** is a veteran of the Indonesian war. He fought with other Dutch troops against Sukarno's independence movement, a losing battle that ended in 1949 when the Dutch had to give up control of this lucrative colony. He now lives in Nanaimo, British Columbia.

---

# The Dutch in Wartime series

### Book 1
### *Invasion*

Edited by:
Tom Bijvoet

90 pages paperback
ISBN: 978-0-9868308-0-8

### Book 2
### *Under Nazi Rule*

Edited by:
Tom Bijvoet

88 pages paperback
ISBN: 978-0-9868308-3-9

### Book 3
### *Witnessing the Holocaust*

Edited by:
Tom Bijvoet

96 pages paperback
ISBN: 978-0-9868308-4-6

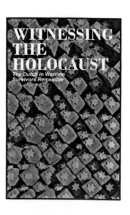

## Book 4
## *Resisting Nazi Occupation*

Edited by:
Anne van Arragon Hutten

108 pages paperback
ISBN: 978-0-9868308-4-6

## Book 5
## *Tell your children about us*

Edited by:
Anne van Arragon Hutten

104 pages paperback
ISBN: 978-0-9868308-6-0

*Keep your series complete: order on-line
at www.dutchinwar.com,
or contact Mokeham Publishing.*

CPSIA information can be obtained
at www.ICGtesting.com
Printed in the USA
FFOW05n1642130415

9 780986 830877